THE READER RESPONSE NOTEBOOK

NCTE Editorial Board

The Reader Response Notebook

Teaching toward Agency, Autonomy, and Accountability

Ted Kesler
Queens College, City University of New York

NATIONAL COUNCIL OF TEACHERS OF ENGLISH
1111 W. KENYON ROAD, URBANA, ILLINOIS 61801-1096
WWW.NCTE.ORG

Staff Editor: Bonny Graham
Interior Design: Jenny Jensen Greenleaf
Cover Design: Pat Mayer

NCTE Stock Number: 38403; eStock Number: 38410
ISBN 978-0-8141-3840-3; eISBN 978-0-8141-3841-0

Library of Congress Cataloging-in-Publication Data

Names: Kesler, Ted, author.
Title: The reader response notebook : teaching toward agency, autonomy, and
    accountability / Ted Kesler.
Description: Urbana, Illinois : National Council of Teachers of English, [2018] | Includes
    bibliographical references and index.
Identifiers: LCCN 2018021522 (print) | LCCN 2018034058 (ebook) | ISBN 9780814138410
    (ebook) | ISBN 9780814138403 | ISBN 9780814138403 (pbk) | ISBN 9780814138410
    (eISBN)
Subjects: LCSH: Reading (Elementary)—United States. | Language arts (Elementary)—
    United States. | English language—Composition and exercises—Study and teaching
    (Elementary)—United States. | Reader-response criticism.
Classification: LCC LB1576 (ebook) | LCC LB1576 .K456 2018 (print) | DDC
    372.4—dc23
LC record available at https://lccn.loc.gov/2018021522

This book is dedicated to my mom,
Dr. Regina Rachel Chanowicz Kesler, 1926–1973.
She taught me to serve communities
graciously, patiently, lovingly.

Contents

Foreword: The Value of Reader Response in a Text-Dominated World

KATHY G. SHORT, *University of Arizona*

John Dewey (1938) argued that we live in an either/or society where educational movements often swing from one extreme to another. He believed that educators are better served by getting off the pendulum and pursuing possibilities that go beyond oppositional extremes. Rosenblatt (1938) took up Dewey's call and rejected the dichotomy of text *or* reader, arguing that reading is a transaction of text *and* reader coming together to create something new, an understanding that goes beyond either one—and changes both. This rejection of opposition lies at the core of the experiences with reader response notebooks shared in this book. These notebooks encourage students to immerse themselves into the fictional and informational story worlds of literature while thoughtfully considering those worlds. They are also a demonstration of how to move beyond the current pendulum swing that rejects the reader in favor of the text through the guise of "close reading."

Current state and national standards and basal reading programs emphasize close reading of texts, recommending that students find and cite evidence in the text. Textual analysis is viewed as bringing rigor to reading. Any text read to or by students is used for instructional purposes, to teach something. If students respond to a text by talking about connections to their lives, teachers are advised to steer them back to the task of talking about the text. Text-dependent questions and evidence, not connection, are valued.

This focus on close textual reading is based in misunderstandings about reader response, specifically that reader response stays at a simple level of personal connections that do not lead to critical thinking or textual analysis. Although reader response does begin with personal connections and interpretations, readers are encouraged to move into an analysis of their responses through dialogue based on evidence from their lives and the text to develop their interpretations. Rosenblatt (1938) argued that students need to first respond as human beings and share their experiences of a story *before* a text is used to teach. Literature is not written to teach a strategy but to illuminate life. The first questions to consider are, "What are you thinking? What connections did you make?" rather than "What was the text about?" and "How does the text work?" Personal connections and responses are essential, but not sufficient, as readers also need to dialogue about their interpretations, critiquing those interpretations and examining whether they are supported by evidence from their lives and the text.

The examples of children's responses in this book honor Rosenblatt's belief that a reader's first response to a text should focus on the book as an experience of life. The second response moves into close reading as students consider those responses by examining *both* the text and their lives. The reader response notebook strategies, such as "parking lot," provide a means for students to gather their impressions as they read, a first response to a text. Students move from these first responses and initial sharing to more in-depth dialogue, using strategies that encourage them to examine character relationships, key moments, or significant issues through a sketch-to-stretch, web, or Venn diagram.

The Reader Response Notebook also uses strategies such as "the missing voice" and "power meter" to encourage readers to bring a critical lens to their reading, which requires *both* personal response and textual analysis. If readers are engaged only in textual analysis, they do not learn to question the text and the assumptions about society on which the text is based. They circle around within the text, engaging in evaluation but not critique of missing voices or issues of equity and power.

When readers engage in both personal connection and textual analysis, they consider multiple perspectives as a way to critique and challenge what exists in society, to examine who benefits from these inequities, as well as to imagine new possibilities (Freire, 1970). Readers need to go outside the world of the text to challenge that world and bring the text back to their lives to challenge their views. Encouraging readers to engage only in close reading keeps the text distant from their lives—they read as spectators instead of immersing themselves in experiences that connect them to, and take them beyond, their own lives.

Close text-based reading is a return to a narrow definition of what and how we read. History indicates that this type of textual criticism has turned off generations of students because it lacks purpose, meaning, and relevancy to ideas and issues that students care about. Many of us have painful memories of sitting in high school literature classes, struggling to come up with the "right" interpretation of the assigned text and taking a text apart piece by piece, destroying interest in and enjoyment of that text. Our connections and thinking were not valued, and we saw no relevance for that reading in our lives.

Rosenblatt provided a powerful indictment of this approach in 1938 and her critique remains valid today. We do not need to choose between personal connection and textual analysis; the choice is not either/or but both. The risk of ignoring that choice is producing another generation of readers who avoid reading because it is painful school work instead of meaningful life work. *The Reader Response Notebook* put this theory into action by providing concrete examples of the invitations teachers can offer students to unite their lives with the world of the text to build understanding through reflection and dialogue. By redefining close reading from a reader response stance, this book provides a generative means of moving forward as educators who reject either/or pendulums and instead create our own pathways of understanding.

Works Cited

Dewey, J. (1938): *Education and experience.* New York: Collier.
Freire, P. (1970). *Pedagogy of the oppressed.* New York: Herder & Herder.
Rosenblatt, L. (1938). *Literature as exploration.* Chicago: Modern Language Association.

Acknowledgments

I t helped to announce to my various communities that I was writing a book. Community members invariably asked, "How's it going with your book?" and I invariably had to respond that the book was in progress. "Still? Wow, it sure takes a long time." Yes, I know. But I recommend this process to anyone who intends to write a book. By making my intentions public, important people in my life pushed me to a point of no return, and my only choice was to get the book done. Their expectations propelled me past rejections: there was no way I would ever be able to face these people had I given up.

In particular, thank you family members: my brothers, Mark and David; my sister, May; my dad, Michael; my mother-in-law, Rose Weinberg; my sister-in-law, Elana Weinberg. Then, a special thank you to my immediate family: my wife, Judy; my daughter, Korina; my son, Daniel; and my dog, Pilpel. They keep me grounded. You can never get too esoteric when you still need to walk the dog, take out the garbage, and sweep the kitchen floor. Most of all, they provide an undercurrent of love that enables my steady writing routine.

Thanks to Kurt Austin, who first saw the possibilities of this book when I presented the idea in an email and encouraged me to go forth with it. Thanks to the reviewers of the proposal and manuscript, who provided helpful feedback that inevitably improved the manuscript. Thanks to Kathy Short, who read the manuscript, gave me her endorsement, and wrote such a beautiful foreword. Thanks to Bonny Graham for making the final stages of book production creative and fun.

Thanks to my third-grade students, now adults, from the Special Music School in New York City. I feature some of their work in this book. They affirmed the creativity and thoughtfulness that was possible with a reader response notebook. Thanks as well to my graduate preservice students at Queens College. They lifted "just another course assignment" to life work. Their ingenuity inspired me to revisit this work with elementary school children.

Finally, thanks to the team at P.S. 144Q: Reva Gluck-Schneider, principal extraordinaire; second-grade teacher Jen Sussman; third-grade teacher Lori Diamond; fourth-grade teachers Deb Kessler and Lauren Heinz; and fifth-grade teacher Lesley Doff. A special thanks to all their wonderful students during the years of this project. Obviously, the work that this book presents was only possible because of their exuberant commitment. They all, students and teachers both, took the ideas I presented and ran with them, producing results that far exceeded my expectations. It was the need to share publicly that the remarkable work they demonstrated was possible that made me determined to write this book. Thank you all!

Introduction:
Origins as a Classroom Teacher

As a classroom teacher in New York City public elementary schools, I taught my students to write responses in a reader response notebook (RRN). Figure 1 was a typical student response, this one by Ethan, one of my third graders. Not bad. Ethan addressed a theme in *Uncle Jed's Barbershop* (Mitchell & Ransome, 1998) and connected it to our read-aloud book, *The Wheel on the School* (DeJong, 1972), citing a piece of evidence from the former. My students' entries included summaries or responses to prompts about the main character, character relationships, or the most important part of the story. But their responses usually came at the *end* of reading, or what Hancock (1993) calls retrospective accounts. In addition, my students knew that I was the only one who read their notebooks and that I read them for the primary purpose of monitoring their reading and assessing their understanding. What happened to students who were reluctant or resistant writers, or who did not represent their best thinking about the texts they read in writing?

I wanted my students' responses to be more fluid, reflecting the messy process of constructing understanding during reading. I believe interpretation is a recursive process that involves revision of thought, what Hancock (1993) calls an introspective journey. But I also wanted response to reading not to overwhelm reading time; I was aware of the benefits of uninterrupted reading time (Calkins, 2001). So I started teaching and encouraging a broader range of RRN responses during interactive read-aloud and independent reading. Guided by the Reading and Writing Project of Teachers College, which was my source of professional development, I taught students strategies such as sketch-to-stretch, stop-and-jot, representational drawing, or using sticky notes to record thoughts in the margins of their books. When I conferred with students, I encouraged them to use T-charts for text evidence, to keep character lists, or to act as the illustrator, including captions, for books that had few or no illustrations. I taught students to keep ongoing lists in the back of their notebooks of "Books I Want to Read Next" or "Books I Love."

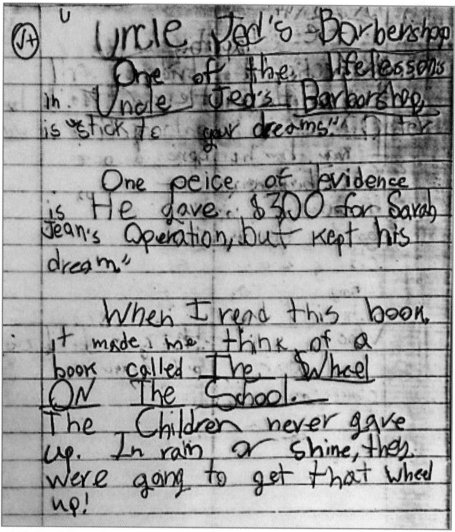

FIGURE 1. An example of student response in a reader response notebook.

During independent reading time, I held a conference with Luiko, one of my third-grade students. She was reading Laura Ingalls Wilder's Little House series. In our conference, Luiko explained that she was trying to picture each scene as she read *On the Banks of Plum Creek* (1937/2008), which made perfect sense. I had been emphasizing "making a movie in your mind" as we read as a way to envision the text. We often practiced this skill during our whole-class read-aloud time. Envisioning is especially important for strong comprehension of historical fiction because setting is such an integral part of the dramatic events. I knew Luiko's artistic propensity. Why not act as the illustrator as she read and pretend that she was hired by the publisher to illustrate the book? What dramatic scenes might she illustrate? She shared two scenes she already had in mind and how she might draw them. She was clearly eager to do this work. I suggested she might include captions to build the connection for the reader from the illustration to the episode in the book.

Figure 2 shows an example of Luiko's reading work as she continued her independent reading. It was clear from her illustrations that she was under-

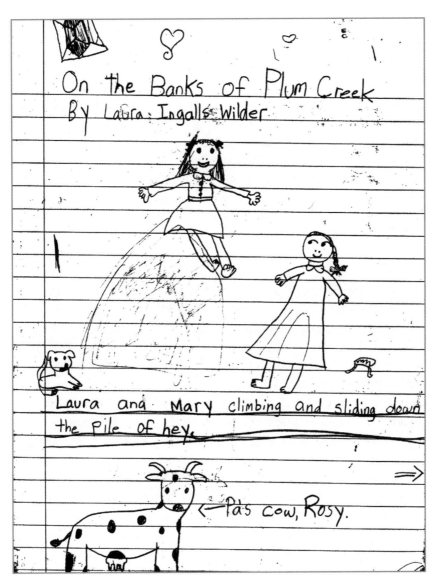

FIGURE 2. A sample of Luiko's drawings for *On the Banks of Plum Creek*.

standing descriptive passages and key events in the book. Her work supported state and national reading standards that expect close reading, citing textual evidence, inferring, determining importance, summarizing, and comprehending complex literary texts independently and proficiently.

I experienced the benefits of opening up the RRN for more introspective thinking using a broad range of responses. When students finished books, their final responses became stronger because of the discussions and reflections on all the entries and other trails of thinking they had engaged in. My students became more deliberate, purposeful, and reflective readers.

Developing a New Vision

In my present position in the Department of Elementary and Early Childhood at Queens College, focusing on literacy and children's literature, I began to explore more possibilities for the RRN with the graduate students in my language and literacy foundation courses. Now informed by theories of semiotic resources, expansive theories about texts and popular culture, and sociocultural practices from my doctoral coursework, I opened up students' reading lives to their favorite TV shows and movies, to songs they loved, to the use of drawing and color, to designing on the page, to co-opting digital forms and formats. Students were generative and imaginative in their notebook responses. The texts they loved were now sanctioned in an academic context for rigorous thinking, and they learned to bring that rigorous and creative thinking to academic texts. They realized there were multiple ways to show in-depth thinking beyond essays. They reported reclaiming their literate lives.

I knew then that I had to revisit the RRN with these new understandings in elementary and middle school classrooms. I brought this work to P.S. 144 in Queens, New York. The principal, Reva Gluck-Schneider, knew me from professional development work I had done when she was a classroom teacher. She introduced me to a group of teachers who epitomize professionalism: Lori Diamond, Lauren Heinz, Debra Kessler, and Lesley Doff. Later, Jennifer Sussman joined this group. These teachers trusted me with their limited instructional time while facing mandates and the demands of standardized tests. They opened up their classrooms and used their lunch period to meet with me each time I visited, on a speculation that their students would be able to use the RRN in the same creative, generative ways my graduate students had discovered if we just made these opportunities available to them. Did I really think elementary and middle school students could do this? I did, these teachers did, and their students proved they could. But even we were surprised by what students could achieve when we truly value this tool for thinking and leading literate lives.

This book reports the amazing discoveries that I and teachers I work with have made so far using this simple, tried-and-true tool, the reader response notebook, in not-so-simple ways. I say "so far" because we continue to investigate and discover issues of serious concern in public education. Our interests so far include: (a) What range of reader responses might elementary and middle school students express if we open up a variety of resources to them? (b) How might we design instruction so students develop autonomy that matches their reading purposes in their use of reader response notebooks? (c) What does this variety of response show about students' reading comprehension? (d) How does broadening what counts as text influence students' literate identities and their development as readers? (e) How might we use their notebooks as tools to develop a literate community of practice? (f) How does this notebook work support students' collaborative discussions and their written responses (e.g., essays), aligned with state and national standards? (g) How might we guide students toward self-assessment of their notebook work? (h) In what ways do these notebooks, used in the ways we are continually developing, become tools for students living literate lives? What we have learned so far is that by opening up what counts as texts and the possibilities of designing on the page, using a wide variety of responses, and by valuing these practices as important literate behaviors, we are expanding what it means to be readers and writers in school settings (Bloome, 1985) and who can join the literacy club (Smith, 1988).

Some Examples

Figure 3 showcases three examples of the generative thinking in students' RRNs from Lesley Doff's fifth-grade class. In Figure 3a, Samantha used a coded message to reveal the motives of Eric, the protagonist in *The Bully Book* (Gale, 2013). In addition to showing impressive attention to detail, Samantha integrated the secret code used for messages that Eric receives and uses throughout the book to solve the mystery of the Bully Book that torments his life. In Figure 3b, Emma imagined a text message exchange between Mr. Collins, the seventh-grade math teacher in *All of the Above* (Pearsall, 2006), and his adult daughter, at a pivotal moment in the story, right after the tetrahedron project with his after-school math club was destroyed. In the book, we know only that Mr. Collins has an adult daughter and a son; we know nothing of his relationship with them. So Emma used a popular social media format to imagine this relationship. In Figure 3c, Elizabeth showed the route that Skelly, who has Alzheimer's, took through the

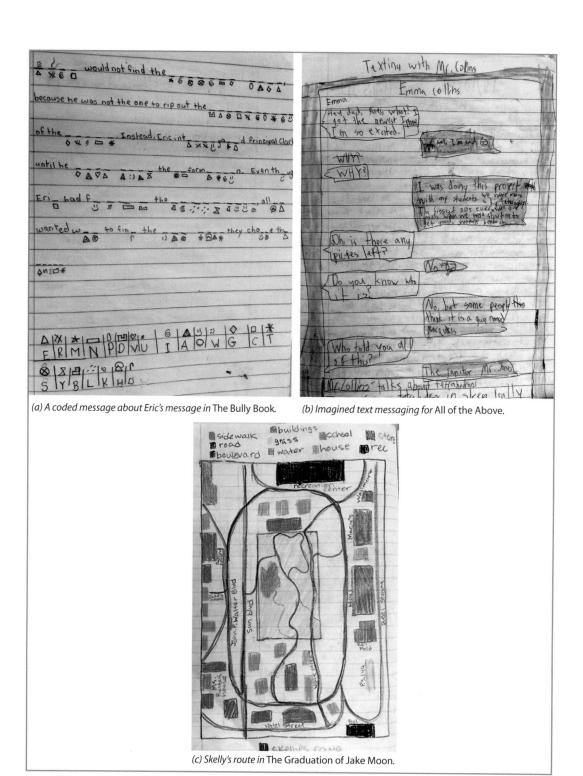

(a) A coded message about Eric's message in The Bully Book.

(b) Imagined text messaging for All of the Above.

(c) Skelly's route in The Graduation of Jake Moon.

FIGURE 3. Examples of generative thinking in RRNs.

town on the night he wandered away from home unattended in *The Graduation of Jake Moon* (Park, 2002). Elizabeth both envisioned the layout of the town and synthesized textual evidence to trace Skelly's route. As in Figure 3b, Elizabeth identified a pivotal moment in the story; she then realized that a map might be the best way to depict the tension and resolution of this event. She purposefully applied resources for mapmaking, such as colors, shapes, symbols, and lines.

Who We Are

In this book, I share how to define, use, and develop the RRN so students can achieve a more creative level of reader response and lead more literate lives. I draw examples from my own third-grade students when I was a New York City public school teacher, from students grades 2–8, in classes that are currently doing this work in New York City public schools, and from my graduate students, who keep RRNs as part of our coursework. I fluctuate between the *I* voice and the *we* voice depending on the scenario I'm describing, to give some sense of my collaboration with teachers for the ideas in this book.

Most examples come from P.S. 144 in Forest Hills, Queens. When I brought this project to Principal Reva Gluck-Schneider in the spring of 2013, she was immediately responsive and quickly assembled an interested group of teachers to consider the project. P.S. 144 has a growing population of students that now exceeds school capacity. Since 2014, fifth graders are in trailer classrooms that take up part of the school playground. During the 2016–17 school year, P.S. 144 had 841 students, preK–grade 5, with one Gifted and Talented (G & T) class for each grade. Fourteen percent of the school population qualified for free or reduced-price lunch. The ethnic makeup of the school was 36 percent Asian, 35 percent White, 18 percent Hispanic, 6 percent Black, 4 percent American Indian, and 1 percent Other. Students with special needs comprised 13 percent of the school population, and 5 percent were English language learners (ELLs). Class size in grades 2 through 5 averaged twenty-eight students. Across two and a half years, from September 2013 through December 2015, I spent one day every two weeks working alongside a self-selected team of teachers with their students. This team included Jen Sussman (grade 2 G & T), Lori Diamond (grade 3 G & T), Lauren Heinz (grade 4), Debra Kessler (grade 4), and Lesley Doff (grade 5 G & T). Before each visit, we would plan the ELA lesson for their students, including use of the RRN, and we held a lunchtime meeting to process the work, problem solve, and decide on next steps. We kept a blog, with satellite blogs for each teacher's class, to share our progress. We presented as a team about this work at the National Council of Teachers of English Annual Convention in both 2014 and 2015.

Summary of the Book

The book follows the trajectory of the reading response notebook work as it unfolds across an academic year. The first chapters describe explicit teaching of RRN strategies that we want all students to know and use. Later chapters demonstrate how students develop agency with the strategies we teach and generate their own; then, through ongoing sharing sessions, they develop autonomy. In Chapter 1, "A New Vision of the Reading Response Notebook," I define the new vision of the RRN that is the focus of this book and how it differs significantly from the more standard uses of the RRN in schools. As well as explaining some of the theories this vision is based on, I present an expanded vision of what counts as a text in school, including popular culture texts. In Chapter 2, "Getting Started," I explain how to launch this work with students, including expanding what counts as texts for students, using reading logs, and teaching a first strategy, all using the gradual release of responsibility model (Duke & Pearson, 2002). I also share students' ongoing lists and how these lists develop their literate identities. In Chapter 3, "Expanding Possibilities," I explore next strategies to teach, using an anchor chart to support students' strategy use. I take you inside classrooms to hear how instruction unfolded for students to accomplish these strategies.

Chapter 4, "Toward Agency, Autonomy, and Accountability," illustrates how we developed and implemented a checklist to support students' independent use of strategies, describing share sessions that promote students' reflective self-assessment, build a community of practice, and stimulate generative and creative responses. I discuss establishing grading criteria that hold students accountable for their work and then share ideas for using these grading criteria in manageable ways. Examples showcase dialogic classroom practices, such as conferring and small-group and whole-class discussions, with the RRN as mediational tool. In Chapter 5, "Permeable Boundaries: Living Literate Lives in and out of School," you will see how the RRN becomes a tool that bridges students' literate practices in and out of school. I share their generative responses that co-opt popular culture and social media formats, as well as school-based response formats for popular culture texts. The playfulness and flexibility that arises empowers students' literate identities. Chapter 6, "Changing Lives," features students' reflections on how this notebook work helps form their identities as literate beings, and I consider what their responses suggest for our work as teachers. I also share teachers' reflections of how this work is transforming their literacy teaching practices. Finally, I share some thoughts of next steps in our own journey using RRNs. Each chapter demonstrates how this work addresses and expands state and national standards expectations for excellent teaching and learning in the English language arts. In the appendixes, I provide anchor charts and grading forms. So—let's begin the journey.

A New Vision of the Reader Response Notebook

What Is a Reader Response Notebook?

You are likely familiar with a reader response notebook (RRN). A reader response notebook is a bound school notebook of 100 to 200 pages, although some students may opt to purchase cloth- or leather-bound journals. We require bound pages so that students don't tear pages out and so the pages have more permanence than those in a spiral notebook or three-ring binder. As with writer's notebooks, we encourage students to personalize the covers of their RRNs with favorite quotes, images of covers of their favorite books, pictures of their perfect reading spots, and so on (see Figure 4).

FIGURE 4. Dyandra's reading response notebook cover.

Beyond the physical format, a reader response notebook is a tool for thinking about texts our students read. Vygotsky (1978) states that all people engage in goal-directed activities using mediational means that are both signs and tools. Language, of course, is the dominant sign system. In the case of the RRN, the goal-directed activities are reader responses to texts. The RRN enables blending of tools and symbol systems, including language, to achieve higher mental functioning.

When I first brought up my vision of the RRN as a tool for thinking, Reva Gluck-Schneider, the principal of P.S. 144 in Queens, New York, asked, "Why not just use digital tools such as a blog or some of the great apps that are available such as Wordle or Glogster or VoiceThread?" Her school was moving in the direction of integrating technology into classroom instruction. Although the integration and evolution of digital technologies in classrooms is occurring so rapidly that it's impossible to keep up, digital technologies are expanding what's possible for reader response in powerful ways (see, for example, Kesler, Gibson, & Turanksy, 2016).

The physical RRN has an important place among these digital tools. It's portable, accessible, and doesn't rely on electricity or internet access or subscription. Students can simply take out their RRNs whenever they want or need to respond to a text. Even today, not all classrooms have one-to-one digital devices, and even if they do, not all devices are always charged or working properly. We and our students have to contend with the vagaries of internet connection and access; often, some sites are blocked by the school router system. Moreover, not all students, particularly students of low socioeconomic backgrounds, have digital devices or internet access outside of school (Leu, Forzani, Rhoads, Maykel, Kennedy, & Timbrell, 2015). Because the RRN is both physical and bound, teachers and students are able to easily track, reflect on, and revisit entries and monitor progress.

Some Common Views of Reader Response Notebooks

In my extensive work as a staff developer in elementary and middle schools around the country, I have noticed patterns in the use of RRNs. Sometimes students copy the aim or goal of the lesson in the notebook, perhaps including an explanation. For example, "Good readers learn new vocabulary words by using context clues," followed by an explanation. Students then provide some examples of using context clues to figure out new vocabulary in their reading. Another pattern I notice is summarizing the chapter or article. A third pattern is responding to prompts or reading skills the class is focusing on, such as writing about the central conflict, drawing conclusions, or using text evidence from two or more texts to answer a question that the text set addresses, such as "Why are elephants being poached in central Africa, and what can be done about it?" Some teachers assign intermediary steps that guide students toward this complex response, such as focusing on one text at a time or using graphic organizers or thinking maps to collect evidence and then develop reasons and notice patterns across texts. Some teachers also provide paragraph frames (Cudd & Roberts, 1989) to support students' responses, especially to nonfiction texts.

There are some compelling reasons for these patterns of response. First, they value expository writing, which is a mode of communication students need to develop. Developing strong expository writing skills also addresses state and national ELA standards. These responses also prepare students for state standardized ELA tests, which are intended to be aligned with standards.

But you might also recognize some compelling limitations to these patterns of response:

1. Responses are predominantly teacher assigned, and the teacher is often the only intended audience. Consequently, students don't develop a sense of ownership of their responses, nor a sense of purpose beyond pleasing the teacher. (How often do you see students willingly, without prompting, write a summary of a text they read?)

2. The teacher is usually the sole assessor of students' responses. This develops more dependency on the teacher, evidenced by comments such as "Am I done?" "Did I do a good job?" "What do we do when we finish?"

3. The emphasis on primarily written responses prevents other modes of expression. We all know students who would benefit from expressing themselves and their learning in different ways, especially when our goal is to develop and enable deep comprehension of texts. Günther Kress (2000), a social semiotic theorist, laments (2000): "The single, exclusive and intensive focus on written language has dampened the full development of all kinds of human potentials" (p. 156).

4. Some of these same students are reluctant or vulnerable readers and writers (Jaeger, 2015; Johnson, 2014). By privileging predominantly written forms, and mostly expository writing, we hinder their opportunities to access and develop deeper levels of comprehension. Writing scholars such as Thomas Newkirk (2009) and Tom Romano (2013) explain how state and national standards further exacerbate this emphasis on expository responses by devaluing literary writing. For example, there is no mention in national or state writing standards of poetry or drama, nor any gesture

toward hybrid or multigenre writing. Romano laments: "The [s]tandards want writing that's all head, no heart" (p. 189).

5. Expository responses often require substantial amounts of time, especially if they are done thoughtfully. We must consider the amount of time these kinds of written responses require at the expense of students' reading (Bomer, 2011; Calkins, 2001).

6. Most of these responses are retrospective accounts of reading (Hancock, 1993). In other words, students respond *after* reading the text. Limiting responses to after reading denies students opportunities to develop their thinking *during* reading, or what Hancock (1993) calls introspective journeys.

How Can We Help Develop Students' Thinking *during* Reading?

Randy Bomer, in *Building Adolescent Literacy in Today's English Classrooms* (2011), Lucy Calkins, in *The Art of Teaching Reading* (2001), and Irene C. Fountas and Gay Su Pinnell, in *Guiding Readers and Writers, Grades 3–6* (2001), provide ideas that develop more autonomy, more student choice, and more opportunities for introspective journeys of thought that occur *during* reading in dialogic classroom communities. They all argue against the "commodification of knowledge" (Bomer, 2011, p. 120), or the display of knowledge, mostly for teachers' purposes of assessing students' comprehension and holding them accountable. Instead, they value exploratory writing as a journey of thought, in preparation for writing for an audience (e.g., literary essays) or for discussion. They all prioritize opportunities for students to focus on the act of reading itself and minimize other activities around it, thereby encouraging teachers and students to use reading response strategies efficiently, purposefully, and only in ways that extend and develop meaning making.

Educators such as Aimee Buckner (2009) at the elementary school level, Linda Rief (2007) at the middle school level, and Tom Romano (2013) at the high school level have also provided copious ideas for reading notebook responses. Rief especially emphasizes the use of sketching and drawing, encouraging students to apply a wide array of drawing tools for expressing their ideas. She chooses to combine reading and writing notebook work as two sides of the same coin: to enable a more fluid interchange of ideas between students' reading and writing work. Romano is especially known for multigenre writing, encouraging students to respond to one text through multiple genres: for example, writing a letter from one character to another, writing a dramatic scene as a script for readers theater, writing from another character's perspective, writing a "missing" scene, turning a text into a poem or a song, and so on. A set of multigenre responses connects to provide new insights into a text. These authors demonstrate that, by opening up what's possible for reader response, we open up opportunities for students' expression and for developing deeper understandings of the texts they read. I am mindful of Rief's (2007) wise advice for students: "What's important is they are noticing the world. They are making connections. They are asking questions. They are participating by thinking" (p. 35). In this book, you'll see examples of how these educators' ideas have influenced the RRN work I guide students to do.

A New Vision for Reader Response Notebooks

Building on this reading response work, I emphasize three other elements that contribute to a new vision for reading response notebooks. First, I encourage "designing on the page" that welcomes a wide array of writing and drawing resources. Second, I expand what counts as a text, including popular culture media. Third, I emphasize the sociocultural context of classroom literacy practices that supports students' generative responses in their RRNs. Most of all, in the following pages, I show the application of these three elements using a systemic approach that guides students toward agency, autonomy, and accountability.

Designing on the Page

In *Creating Classrooms for Authors and Inquirers*, Kathy G. Short and Jerome C. Harste (1996) state, "Literacy is much broader than language" (p. 14). They define *literacy* as "the processes by which we, as humans, mediate the world for the purpose of learning" (p. 14). We mediate the world through socially embedded sign systems, or modes, such as dance, music, mathematics, art, or writing. They explain that a literate person is someone who flexibly uses multiple modes to clearly explore, articulate, and communicate ideas within a community of practice that recognizes and values these forms of expression, whether the expression takes the form of a dance, a drawing, a mathematical formula, a poem, an essay, a song, another form, or some combination of these forms.

As a bound notebook, the RRN has both affordances and constraints (Jewitt & Kress, 2003). One of its constraints is that reader response is confined to composing on bound, regular-sized, lined paper. Too often we further limit students' responses to essay-like notebook entries. This constraint limits all the multimodal ways that students might express meaning in response to texts they read. Conversely, one of the affordances of the RRN is that it allows designing on the page. As teachers, we can make accessible to students drawing tools such as markers, colored pencils and pens, pastels, and crayons. Elliot Eisner (1998), a scholar of arts in education, has stated, "What we come to know about the world is influenced by the tools we have available" (p. 28). By making drawing tools accessible, we also value students' composing processes, or students' introspective journeys (Hancock, 1993), over "pencil-centered" responses that emphasize correctness (Leigh, 2010), or what Hancock called "retrospective accounts." We can encourage students' choice of drawing tools, their deliberate use of color, their drawings and use of symbols, as well as their choices for layout of drawings and words and their design of fonts for their writing. Students' intentions in their choice of tools and colors and design become part of their meaning-making process (Albers, 2007). So, in addition to words, elements of design expand how students can express meaning on each page.

Other affordances include the multiple kinds of writing students can do in addition to traditional expository essay-like responses. Figure 5 is a list of the kinds of writing students have done in their RRNs. When combined with design elements, then, the RRN affords unlimited possibilities for response.

Short and Harste (1996) discuss *transmediation*, a concept first developed by Suhor (1984). Transmediation is the process of transforming the meaning in one sign system, such as language, into another sign system, such as drawing. Since there is no ready-made equivalent across modes, the communicator faces anomalies and must think generatively to re-present the content. This generative thinking propels the creator to think metaphorically and is at the core of meaning making. Short and Harste (1996) explain that as teachers, "we need to learn to look beyond the surface of the text to the deep meaning if we are to take

- Essays
- Poems
- Song lyrics
- Lists
- Scripts
- Letters
- Signs
- Notes
- Fan fiction
- Writing in the voices of characters
- Clippings from newspapers, magazines, ticket stubs, programs, brochures
- Social media formats, such as instant messaging, a Facebook page, Twitter feeds, Instagram posts
- Flow maps, Venn diagrams, T-charts, timelines, webs, diagrams, maps, and other visual displays
- Mathematical symbols, computer codes, game codes, musical notation, secret messages, symbol systems from other languages (e.g., Japanese, Hebrew, Arabic), and other symbol systems
- Various forms of writing: postcards, thinking and dialogue bubbles, labels

FIGURE 5. Kinds of writing in students' RRNs.

children and their early involvement in literacy as seriously as is merited" (p. 21).

The drawing by my third-grade student Gabrielle in Figure 6 shows transmediation in action. During our whole-class read-aloud, *The Wheel on the School* (DeJong, 1972), I asked my students to sketch the scene that is described in approximately four pages in Chapter 4 (pp. 63–66) of Janus guarding his precious cherry tree, the only fruit tree in his seaside town in Holland, where the story takes place. Gabrielle's sketch shows such thorough understanding of this scene. She wrote the title of the book and a caption for her sketch, "Janice under the chery [sic] tree guarding it." She depicts grumpy old Janus with only stumps for legs in his wheelchair holding a rope with tin scraps tied to it to make a clattering sound when he shakes it to scare the

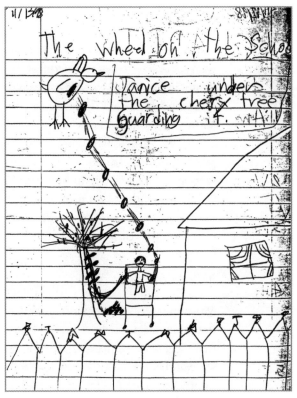

FIGURE 6. Gabrielle's sketch of Janus under the cherry tree.

birds away. The partial view of his house indicates that Janus is in the backyard. In the branches of the tree are the cherries. Next to Janus's wheelchair is a pile of stones. Gabrielle drew the sharp, high fence around Janus's property with its nails and jagged, broken pieces of glass bottles on top of each point, like barbed wire, to prevent the boys from climbing over whenever Janus wasn't around.

The trajectory shows Janus hurling a stone at a magpie—the one bird "bold enough and clever enough to raid the tree and steal a cherry in spite of all the rattling and banging and clatter" (p. 64). This action makes sense when we learn, on page 65: "At boy or bird, Janus let fly, and through the years his aim had become deadly." But how do you represent this deadly aim in a picture? This was an anomaly that Gabrielle had to solve. She had to transmediate descriptive phrases such as "hurl a stone" and "let fly" and "his aim had become deadly" (p. 65) into the grammar system of drawing. In our sociocultural context, Gabrielle knew that in pictures, an artist might use a form of stop-action animation. So she depicted a series of stones, connected by jagged parallel lines that finally connect to the bird, to express contact.

Overall, Gabrielle's drawing was a grand synthesis of four pages of description. Moreover, her self-correction of *G* to *g* in *guarding* in the caption shows Gabrielle's attention to proofreading. It was clear that students such as Gabrielle were able to show strong comprehension with few words and the use of the visual mode. This awareness was a relief to students who were reluctant writers and to me because I was able to provide alternative ways for these students to show their comprehension without relying exclusively on written explanations.

If you value designing on the page in the RRN, you need to open up the possibilities for students' choice of kinds of writing and materials for reader response. This will expand the meaning that students are able to express (Leigh, 2010). This means you need to give permission and teach into students' use of pens, pencils, crayons, Cray-Pas, markers, collage, choice of color and font, layout, and other design elements.

What Counts as a Text

Multimodality also expands what counts as a text. A text isn't just school-sanctioned material, such as a trade book, or a passage in an anthology, or an article in a weekly newsmagazine, or the recommended texts for each grade level that state and national standards specify. A text is any coherent organization of signs in any mode or modal ensemble that communicates meaning to an audience. A text, then, can be a painting, a movie, a dance, a chapter book, a photograph, a TV show. Moreover, while our flexible use of reading strategies depends on the particular text and context we are transacting with, we do similar interpretive work for any text: taking a stance, determining importance, making connections, inferring meanings, synthesizing details, asking questions, striving for answers, determining structural elements, deriving themes, and supporting our ideas with textual evidence (RAND Reading Study Group, 2002). This means that in the RRN, I am intent on valuing students' responses to all manner of texts, and if they can develop strong thinking for any text, they can carry those habits of mind over to the more academic texts sanctioned by state and national standards. This is a process that Short and Harste (1996) call "building from the known."

My expansive view of texts also embraces popular culture. Dolby (2003) states: "Popular culture is a more significant, penetrating pedagogical force in young people's lives than schooling" (p. 264). Both Dyson (2003b) and Dolby (2003) explain that students engage in social affiliations that form their identities through agentive actions with popular culture, and these actions are inherently educational. According to Dyson, learning occurs through a process of *recontextualization*. In other words, students appropriate and reframe the symbolic materials from these popular culture resources for their own playful and productive purposes that, if we allow, converge with school-based literacy practices. Our charge as educators, then, is not to shut the school doors to students' participation in popular cultural practices. Both Dyson and Dolby advocate opening up classroom spaces and acting as ethnographers to study how students use popular culture texts for affiliation, pleasure, and agency. We then might create a permeable curriculum that builds bridges to academic literate behaviors and practices. To teach toward democracy, Dolby notes, we "must start within the core of people's dreams and desires, and from where people are, even if they are at the mall" (p. 276).

A Sociocultural Context for Literacy Learning

Vygotsky (1978) asserts that higher mental functioning and human action in general are mediated by tools and signs within specific sociocultural contexts. Wertsch (1991) explains: "It is the sociocultural situatedness of mediated action that provides the essential link between the cultural, historical, and institutional setting on the one hand and the mental functioning of the individual on the other" (p. 48). This social situatedness of mediated action also constructs students' literate identities. Short and Harste (1996) claim, "No one becomes literate without personal involvement in literacy" (p. 14), and so we must "trust learners and the learning process" (p. 15). Students must connect their emerging identities to collaborative classroom practices "as they continually seek understandings of personal and social significance" (p. 60) for living literate lives. This means that students' RRN work is not between each student and the teacher. Rather, each student's RRN work is shaped and developed within a community of practice as all students strive to join the literacy club (Smith, 1988). Students become *accountable* to their community of practice. As students share their responses, they expect what Louise Rosenblatt (1995) calls "warrantable interpretations" from one another.

Johnston (2004) asserts that creating a dialogic classroom community prepares students to lead literate lives. How? In a dialogic classroom, students learn to act strategically by facing choices for solving problems and accomplishing purposeful tasks, thereby developing a sense of *agency.* Agentive readers are not passive; rather, they are active and often transformative in the ways they transact with and use texts. A dialogic community establishes an inquiry stance that values revision of thought and recursive processes, such as changing our minds, elaborating or deleting ideas, and approaching problems in a variety of ways. It values resiliency and flexibility as students solve problems and develop responses that are socially and personally meaningful and emotionally satisfying. These values develop students' autonomy for RRN work, or the abilities to make choices, act purposefully on their choices, and derive pleasure from the process and products of their actions. These are the values I emphasize for students' RRN work.

Summary

Overall, Short and Harste's (1996) construction of reader response is freeing and provides expansive possibilities for all kinds of students to generate insightful responses to all kinds of texts they encounter in the world. If students can generate meaningful responses using more resources to an expansive range of texts, surely more students in our classrooms will experience the benefits of joining the literacy club (Smith, 1988). Like the researchers cited in this chapter, I want to make sure that reader response is a process of thinking our way through texts, an introspective journey "for the capture of these shifting, sometimes colliding, continually developing thoughts" (Hancock, 1993, p. 336). Like Bomer (2011), Calkins (2001), and Fountas and Pinnell (2001), I want to organize these responses in an easily accessible, portable, self-contained notebook. But I also want to open up reader response to designing on the page with a broad range of materials (Albers, 2007; Leigh, 2010) and opportunities to value and respond to a wide range of texts. Moreover, I want the notebook to become an active tool in the sociocultural dynamics of the classroom community of practice. Finally, I want the notebook to be a tool for guiding all students to live literate lives way beyond their time in school by developing habits of agency, autonomy, and accountability. This is an ambitious and transformative agenda to bring to our classroom literacy practices.

Getting Started

Exploring What Texts Are with Students

For students to eventually develop autonomy and agency in their use of the reader response notebook, we first lay a foundation with deliberate, explicit instruction in a few practices and strategies. This instruction enables students' generative practices to develop (emphasized in Chapters 3, 4 and 5). In this chapter, I first describe exploring and expanding what counts as text with students. Next, I provide ideas for implementing reading logs (or digital forms of reading logs) as an integral part of joining the literacy club. I then introduce a pedagogical approach for teaching foundational reading response strategies and share four of these strategies (I share more of them in Chapter 3). I end the chapter with suggestions for ongoing lists and why these lists matter for leading literate lives.

Exploring Popular Culture with Eighth Graders

I stand in front of nine eighth graders in a self-contained class with their teacher, Mr. Nolan. On the whiteboard, I write the following definition of popular culture: "Everyday culture in which both the producer of a text and the audience have knowledge and power over a text's meaning" (Hagood, Alvermann, & Heron-Hruby, 2010, p. 14; for a full exploration of this work, see Kesler, Tinio, and Nolan, 2016). We read it out loud. "So, what does this mean?" I'm met with blank stares, bodies leaning back in chairs, hands scrawling in notebooks. "It sounds kinda complicated, but we can figure this out," I assure them. "Let's take just the first phrase," and I underline *everyday culture*. "So, what TV shows or movies or YouTube videos do you like to watch? What music do you listen to? What sports do you follow? What video games do you play?" Chairs go back on the floor, faces lift, students look at one another with expressions asking, *For real? Is he really letting us talk about this?* They are distrustful. In all their years of schooling, these topics were always off-limits. They were always told to stop talking and get back to work. They had to save these discussions for lunchtime. "Mr. Nolan, what're some of your favorite shows and movies and music?"

"Oh, I loved *The Dark Knight* [the Batman movie]. The Joker was insane and scary. I love watching *Family Guy.* That's usually what I turn to after my daughter's asleep. And you all know what a huge Mets and New York Islanders fan I am."

"Yeah!" some of the students grumble, because they have heard about his sports teams every day. Indeed, there is Islanders and Mets paraphernalia on display around the classroom.

But students' talk is now starting to bubble up. "The Mets is whack! The Yankees rule!" "I love *Family Guy,* too!" "I love *The Simpsons*!" "I seen <u>all</u> the Batman movies!"* So Mr. Nolan and I start circulating from group to group, joining in, like a natural "lunchtime" conversation.

"I <u>still</u> watch *Hannah Montana.* My baby sister loves it!"* Selena exclaims.

"Oh, my daughter loves that show," I add.

At another group: "You ever play *Batman* on PlayStation?"

"No. I don't got that one. But I play *Call of Duty* at my cousin's."

When Mr. Nolan and I reconvene the class, we share the popular culture everyone talked about. On the whiteboard, I write down the categories that arose: magazines, TV shows, movies, music, websites, video games, trading cards (e.g., Magic: The Gathering), books.

"Let's take a look at the next part of our popular culture quote," I say. I underline the phrase *both the producer of a text and the audience have knowledge and power over a text's meaning.* Assuming a thoughtful posture, I muse, "Hmm, I wonder what they [Hagood et al., 2010] mean by that?" I pause. "You know, I have friends who go on Facebook every day, sometimes a few times a day. I don't. I check out Facebook three or four times a week, and never for more than twenty minutes each time. I always feel like I could get stuck in it and it then keeps me from getting other things done. I have some friends who don't use Facebook at all. They tell me, 'I would rather just share my news directly with the people who matter to me, and I don't want my news to be everybody's business.' My own kids don't use Facebook at all. My daughter, Korina, uses Instagram, <u>a lot</u>. I mean, her phone is always binging whenever she gets a new post from one of her Instagram friends." The students are now signaling that they're following me, saying to one another things like, "Oh, I use Instagram too!" "My mom's on Facebook all the time." "I told my moms to stop posting pictures of me!"

---

*In transcriptions, <u>underline</u> means emphasis.

"My daughter told me the other day, 'Facebook's for old people.' She meant me!" I say. They all laugh.

"It's true!" Andre smiles. "Ain't no way I'm usin' it if my moms and aunts and uncles are all on it! I wanna post only with my <u>friends</u>."

"So, what choices do you all make when you use popular culture?" I ask.

Once again students are off, speaking and laughing and smiling. "My dad loves R & B. I call it ol' school." Dwight starts singing, "Talkin' 'bout my girl, my girl." "He starts singin' along, shakin' his hips, and I'm thinkin', 'O, Lord!' but you know, deep down, I like that sound too. I jus' don't let him know." Carmen starts sharing all the Latin music she listens and sings along to: Shakira, Marc Anthony, Romeo Santos.

When I have the students' attention again, I return to the quote by Hagood et al. "Wow! You all clearly make choices about how you use popular culture." Mr. Nolan and I share some examples we overheard. "Who knew? You all have so much knowledge and power over what all these texts mean to you and how you use them!" The students are now beaming with confidence, hearing their own competence as text users praised.

I next distribute a worksheet titled "My Pop Cultural Interests." I demonstrate my own pop culture interests by listing some of my favorite movies, music, magazines, and other texts. Then each student fills out the worksheet (see Figures 7a and b). Mr. Nolan and I ask students to identify as male or female, and we discuss definitions of race, including the terms *biracial* and *multiracial,* in case students want to express racial identities. We elicit common racial categories and invite students to indicate more than one. Our thinking is that indicating race, with the invitation to list more than one, might open up this activity for these eighth graders to also consider sources of cultural differences.

After quietly filling out the worksheet, students share in small groups. We instruct them to pay attention to commonalities and differences and what accounts for both. Students notice how much popular culture they have in common but also popular culture that is based in cultural differences. Each student's worksheet is truly a profile of that person, displaying the distinctive dimensions of his or her engagement with texts in the world. Andre, for example, loves McDonald's but also the Jamaican jerk chicken that his mother prepares. Carmen loves the rock band Green Day but also loves singing along to her favorite Spanish musicians. We then ask students to identify a few (three to five) favorite texts on their worksheets. We list the following guiding questions on the whiteboard:

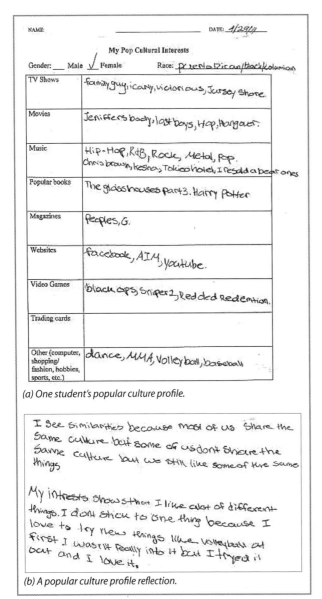

(a) One student's popular culture profile.

> I see similarities because most of us share the same culture but some of us don't share the same culture but we still like some of the same things
>
> My interests shows that I like a lot of different things. I don't stick to one thing because I love to try new things like volleyball at first I wasn't really into it but I tryed it out and I love it.

(b) A popular culture profile reflection.

FIGURE 7. Example of a popular culture profile and profile reflection.

- What do you like about this text?
- Why do you like this text better than other texts?
- Who do you share this text with?
- What don't you like about this text?
- Who might not like this text? Why?

Now that these eighth graders understand that all kinds of texts count as texts, Anthony shares in a small group about his Magic: The Gathering (MTG) cards, explaining the different parts of a card, the value of different cards, how to build a deck, and how to play. He has some cards that are worth more than a hundred dollars! He follows the MTG YouTube channel to learn strategies. On some Saturdays, he plays in all-day tournaments at a local game store. He had never shared much about these activities in school because it's kind of "geeky." Anthony and his classmates are realizing "how texts function as social [and cultural] practices that show identities, values, beliefs, and social networks" (Hagood et al., 2010, p. 3). Moreover, Anthony's MTG practices involve interpreting the cards, applying strategies, evaluating, categorizing, synthesizing the cards as a deck, assessing his performance, and a host of other thinking skills that apply to academic work. Hagood et al. (2010) assert: "Connecting texts that blur across contexts addresses the educational purposes of acknowledging and building on students' literacies in order to enable them to learn both relevant content and the thinking processes that can lead to productive and fulfilled lives" (p. 2).

Expanding What Counts as Texts with Fourth Graders

I'm standing in the front of Lauren Heinz's class of twenty-eight fourth graders. On the whiteboard, I have written "What's a text?"

"Oh, text messaging," a girl calls out, and gestures with her thumbs tapping on an invisible cell phone.

"So, what happens when you text someone or receive a text?" I ask.

"They read it?"

"Hopefully," I respond, "and hopefully, they understand what your text means, or you understand the text they sent you. So, yes, text messages are a kind of text, but I'm thinking of even more kinds of texts."

"Books?" a boy says, pointing to all the books in their library.

"Sure. I call those texts also, but let's look at what's in your library." I walk over and pull out a few books to show them. "I'm noticing this picture book about pumpkins, and this poetry picture book, and this chapter book, and this graphic novel, and this verse chapter book, and this bin of magazines. . . . Discuss with your table partners what you notice about the texts in your library." Ms. Heinz and I now listen in to students' table discussions.

"There are many kinds of books in our libraries."

"I think that's called _genres_."

"Yeah, like nonfiction or realistic fiction."

"Or poetry."

"Ms. Heinz, is poetry a genre?"

Like many teachers, Ms. Heinz deflects the question: "What do you think?"

"Yes, 'cause it's a kind of writing."

"Not everything in our library is books. What about the magazines?"

After five minutes, I reconvene the class. "So, now what would you say a text is?"

"Any kind of writing," Lillian responds. "It could be a text message or a book or a picture book or a magazine." The class seems to concur and I anticipated this, so now I show them a wordless picture book. "What about this? It has no words but tells a story." I flip through the pages. "Is this a text?"

"Yes," Devin responds, "because it's a book."

"So, does a text have to have writing to be a text?" I ask.

I can feel them thinking about this as they try to revise their definition. Stephanie answers, "No. I guess a text can be anything that people read?" She's tentative. After all, up until now in school, they have thought of reading only as decoding print on a page. Is looking at a wordless picture book considered reading?

"Wow!" I respond. "Let's think about that. So we know a text can be many kinds of books, a text message, or a magazine, which are not books, or a book without words, like a wordless picture book, and what they have in common is they all communicate a message or give information or tell a story to an audience." On the whiteboard under "What's a text?" I write: "any work by an author that we make meaning from."

We continue to expand what counts as a text. On the Smartboard, I display a painting, "Christina's World," by Andrew Wyeth. "What's going on in this painting?" I ask. Students describe how close yet far away the house is, how they wish they could see the woman's face, that it looks like she's stuck there, unable to move. "It's almost like she needs someone to lift her up and help her walk," Samantha says. "Where is everybody?" Alexandra asks.

After some more discussion, pointing to our definition of text, I conclude: "So, Andrew Wyeth filled this painting with meaning, and we, the audience, are also making all this meaning from it." We have similar discussions about a song I play for them, a video we watch together, an email we read, again concluding that they all fit the definition of a text. On the whiteboard, I list all the kinds of texts that seem to fit: emails, short stories, postcards, movies, TV shows, songs, paintings, sculptures, plays, circus performances. "How many of these texts have you made or experienced yourselves?" Students share that they write emails and text messages and short stories. Kisha says, "I write songs," and Julius states, "I use iMovie," and Andres declares, "I make comics." We discuss both receiving and sending texts, and this leads us to realize that we are all both text consumers (i.e., we read texts) and creators (i.e., we compose texts).

"I'm gonna make a web of important texts in my life," I declare, and in the middle of the whiteboard I write and draw a circle around the word *text*. Soon my web expands out to a few favorite TV shows, movies, songs, books, magazines, news sources, plays. On top I write "A Few Important Texts in my Life." Then I get students started on making their own webs. As with the eighth graders, I list some questions that explore the social and cultural dimensions of their engagements:

- What texts do you love?
- Who do you share these texts with? How do you share them?
- Who do you make movies (or comics or drawings) for?
- When do you share?
- What happens to the texts you make?

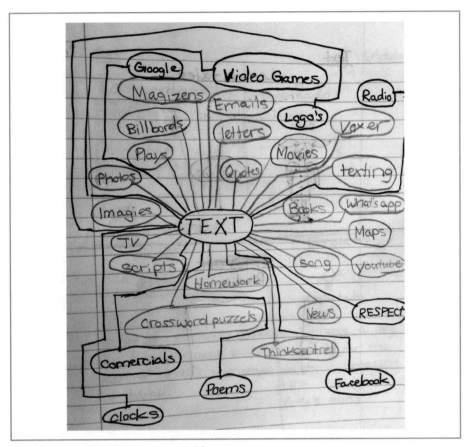

FIGURE 8. Caitlin's web of texts in her life.

Yasly shares, "Well, my mom has posted me singing on her Facebook account, and it got something like 150 likes!"

Figure 8 shows one student's web of texts in her life. After fifteen minutes of work, students are ready to share their webs in their table groups. Our goal—Ms. Heinz's and mine—is to create permeable boundaries between home and school that form bridges to academic literate behaviors and practices (Dyson, 2003b). In later chapters, I provide examples of students' notebook responses to important texts in their lives and the academic literate behaviors these responses demonstrate that we, as teachers, can harness and build on, applying the process that Short and Harste (1996) call "building from the known."

Reading Logs

Even while we value this expansive view of texts, we also, of course, value school-sanctioned books, the kinds of books acknowledged by state and national standards. So one of the beginning-of-the-year practices we teach students, connected to reader response work, is keeping reading logs to monitor their independent reading lives. Excellent websites such as Bookopolis (www.book opolis.com) now expand the purposes and functionalities of reading logs by creating a social network and game elements for reading. But, like all websites, these social reading sites have limitations. For example, they might not locate all books that students search for, or list some awards but not nonfiction book awards, or provide just one format for reading logs. Also, for reasons I mentioned in Chapter 1, you might prefer to continue using paper reading logs. Regardless of your choice of digital or paper media, what truly matters is your and your students' purposeful use of these logs. The reading log should enable both you and your students to realize their habits and preferences in order to reflect on their reading to date and set goals for their future reading.

In my third-grade class, my students kept their current reading log folded inside the back cover of their RRNs (see Figure 9). They put completed logs in my "Completed Work" box and took a new reading log from the tray. I stored completed reading logs in a three-ring binder by alphabetical order of students' last names. In the beginning of the year, I worked with the students on how to write meaningful comments, beyond "I liked it" or "It was good" or "I didn't like it." We came up with ideas such as: use *because* to back up an opinion; say what kind of reader might like this book; give a Wow! fact (for nonfiction books); share one important idea that you learned; write what made the protagonist distinctive; share what you like about this author; focus on the quality of writing; express how this was a new reading experience for you; explain how the book was organized. Once filling out reading logs became habitual in our classroom community, by the end of the first month of school, I told students to take out their current reading logs and I also returned their last completed reading logs. I asked, "What questions can your reading logs answer about your reading habits?" I listed their responses:

- How long am I taking to read a book?
- Am I reading enough pages every day?
- Am I finishing books I started?
- Am I reading across reading levels?
- Am I choosing books that I can understand?

Name: _____

Our 3rd Grade Reading Log

Title	Author	Genre	Date Started	Date Finished	Comment
THE TIME WARP TRIO Summer Reading Is Killing Me!	Jon Scieszka	Humor Fantasy	5/2/01	Deadline 5/28/01 5/24/01	It was extremly funny. I want to read the books they said.
Wanted... Mud Blossom	Betsy Byars	Realistic Fiction Humor	5/24/01	Deadline 6/2/01 5/29/01	I'm happy that Scooty was found.
Armies of Ants	Walter Retan	Animal Non-Fiction	5/30/01	Deadline 5/31/01 5/30/01 early	I learned soooo oooo much about ants! Its alot like Bugs Bugs!
THE NANCY DREW NOTEBOOKS #8 The Best Detective	Carolyn Keene (Illustrated by Anthony Accardo)	Mystery	5/31/01	Deadline 6/3/01 6/5/01	I want to be a detective like Nancy. Bugs!
The Taste Of Black Berries	Doris Buchanan	Realistic Fiction	5/31/01	Deadline 6 days 6/6/01	It shows alot of life lessons.
Micro Monsters	Christopher Maynard	Animal non-fiction	6/5/01	Deadline 6/11/01 6/6/01	There are such cool and amazing pictures.

FIGURE 9. Third-grade reading log.

- Do I have some favorite authors? A favorite series?
- Am I reading many kinds of books?
- Am I writing meaningful comments?
- Am I reading books that other people recommend for me?

In small groups, I then had students discuss their use of reading logs for these guiding questions. They began to realize that their reading logs were for *them,* providing an honest picture of their reading lives in school.

One of the reading habits I valued in my class was a "balanced reading diet": good readers read a balance of different kinds of books. In my class, this meant not just reading many kinds of texts, but also reading across genres and across text complexity. State and national standards acknowledge this value. For example, most standards value reading and evaluating texts in diverse media and formats, closely comparing two or more texts that address similar themes or topics, and proficiently reading and comprehending complex literary and informational texts independently.

Before each marking period, I returned all the reading logs for the term to my students and had them graph the books they had read by genre. On the back of the log, they then wrote five statements about their "balanced reading diet" (see Figures 10a and b). In the first marking period, some students noticed how skewed their reading diets were, usually toward fiction, which meant they often lacked nonfiction or poetry selections. They used this self-awareness to set new independent reading goals, including a more balanced reading diet. Our reading logs then became purposeful tools for reflection and reading development.

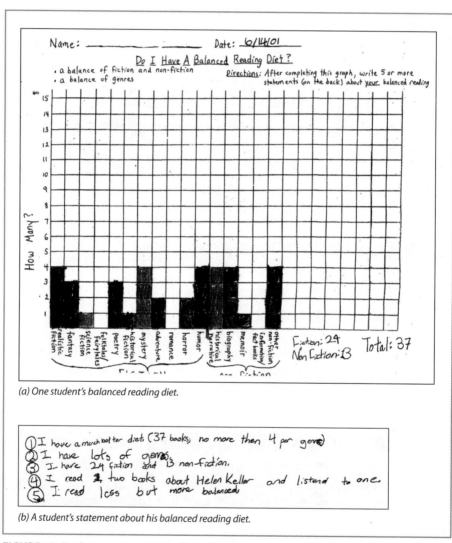

(a) One student's balanced reading diet.

(b) A student's statement about his balanced reading diet.

FIGURE 10. Student responses to their reading "diets."

Teaching Reading Response Strategies

Figure 11 shows the steps of implementation we have used with students, based in the gradual release of responsibility instructional model (Duke & Pearson, 2002). In the first phase and whenever I teach a new strategy, we begin with whole-class practice. I read aloud a short text, such as an engaging picture book (either fiction or nonfiction), essay, poem, feature article, or news report, or I display a compelling work of art. For short texts, I give a copy to each student or to every pair of students. I sometimes retype and copy the text from whatever picture book I'm reading aloud to the class. I demonstrate the new strategy for one excerpt of the text and then send the students off to use the strategy for another part of the text, alone or in partnerships. We then share our work. Sharing of strategies includes sharing with a partner, sharing in small groups, or inviting students who did notable work to share using the document camera. In the beginning of the school year, we mostly teach strategies from Phase 1, as I demonstrate with the sketch-to-stretch strategy in the next section. But even in the beginning of the year, we move fluidly to Phases 2 and 3 through reading conferences, guiding students to try out strategies that we may not yet have taught the whole class but that lay the groundwork for when we do share these strategies more widely, as I demonstrate later in the "Representational Drawing" section. Phase 3 of implementation especially gains momentum as we establish share sessions in our classroom communities, described in the next chapter.

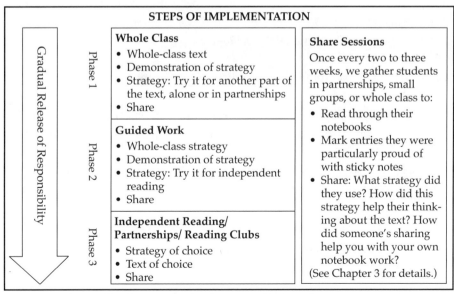

FIGURE 11. Phases of implementation leading toward independence.

Using this gradual release of responsibility model, we deliberately teach students a few starting strategies for their RRNs. In the remainder of this chapter, I describe these starting strategies: *sketch-to-stretch, representational drawing, parking lots, summary boxes and essence chart,* and *lifelong lists.* In Chapter 3, I share several more starting strategies.

Sketch-to-Stretch

One of the first strategies we teach students is *sketch-to-stretch.* In this activity, students create a symbolic sketch that represents for them the theme of a story, or the essence of a character relationship, or the struggle a character faces. We encourage them to use drawing tools, and so all the elements of drawing become resources for meaning making. Short and Harste (1996) explain:

> These engagements encourage students to go beyond a literal understanding of what they have experienced. By becoming involved in this strategy, students who are reluctant to take risks or who have dysfunctional notions of language see that not everyone has the same response to a selection. Although much of the meaning is shared, variations in interpretation add new meanings and new insights.
>
> Often, as students sketch, they generate new insights of their own. They are faced with a problem because the meanings they had constructed for the selection through language cannot be transferred into a sketch. As they deal with this problem, they usually come to understand the selection at a different level than when they first read the book. Sometimes students discuss and explore aspects of meaning they may have captured in art that they were not aware of having understood verbally or musically. (pp. 528–29).

Sketch-to-stretch exemplifies transmediation, a concept introduced in Chapter 1. Basically, because there are no ready-made equivalents as students move from words to pictures, they have to create new ways of representing their thinking. This activity then pushes them to think metaphorically, reaching an interpretive level of textual understanding.

In sketch-to-stretch, it's imperative to begin with a prompt that leads to rhetorical, interpretive responses. Some examples:

- "Draw the relationship between [two characters in the story]."
- "Sketch the central conflict that these characters are facing."
- "Sketch what the character is contending with in his world."
- "How might you show what matters most to this character?"

• "Show how setting influences the events [in this story or between these characters]."

We then tell students to write a caption explaining what their sketch represents. One reason I like to start off with sketch-to-stretch is that students don't need to be talented artists to draw symbolically; they can use lines, shapes, colors, and symbols for their interpretive work. Therefore, all students can feel successful with their response.

In the first session in Deb Kessler's fourth-grade class, students gathered in the meeting area as I read aloud *Stevie* by John Steptoe (1986). After the interactive read-aloud, I guided students to "draw the relationship between Robert and Stevie." I was applying Phase 1: teaching and practicing a response strategy for a whole-class text. I demonstrated my own sketch-to-stretch using thick black and yellow crayons on chart paper. Starting in the upper left corner of a frame, I drew dark black diagonal lines that got lighter as I reached the center of the frame, then used yellow diagonal lines from light to dark as I moved from the center to bottom right corner of the frame. The students were surprised that my sketch-to-stretch didn't show representational drawing, instead relying on symbolic meaning. I discussed my sketch, noticing, as Short and Harste (1996) explain, that I generated meaning for the story in the process of giving my explanation. Furthermore, my explanation prepared me to write my caption. Under my frame, I wrote: "This shows how Robert's attitude toward Stevie moved from anger toward acceptance, and how Stevie brought some light to Robert." We then sent the students off to do their own sketch-to-stretch and then share their work. Figure 12 is Sylvan's response. In Sylvan's sketch-to-stretch, Stevie is looking at Robert imploringly, with outstretched arms. On his T-shirt,

FIGURE 12. Robert is the sun; Stevie is the moon.

Sylvan wrote, "I Want You," emphasizing his neediness. Robert is looking right at us with a crazed face and his hands up in exasperation. On his T-shirt, Sylvan labeled, "Mad Kid in Town." You can see the metaphorical, interpretive thinking that Short and Harste (1996) describe as the power of this strategy at work in Sylvan's response. The moon depends on the sun as its source of light, just as Stevie depends on Robert to shine down upon him for a sense of belonging. For example, in one pivotal scene, it's clear that Robert is angry when he can't join his friends because he has to look after Stevie, and after Robert's friends leave, Stevie says, "I'm sorry, Robert. You don't like me, Robert? I'm sorry."

"Aw, be quiet," Robert replies. "That's okay."

Meanwhile, Sylvan's caption expresses how Robert is mad at Stevie for taking attention away from him, just as the sun may be jealous of the moon glowing brightly in the nighttime sky.

Representational Drawings

When I was a third-grade teacher, students' sketches were an alternative form of formative assessment for me to monitor students' comprehension. In the introduction, I shared Luiko's representational drawings for *On the Banks of Plum Creek* (Wilder, 1937/2008). By acting like an illustrator, Luiko practiced envisioning narrative descriptions of key moments in the narrative, often rereading these passages for details to include in her drawings. In Chapter 1, I shared Gabrielle's representational drawing for our whole-class read-aloud, *The Wheel on the School* (DeJong, 1972), and what it showed about Gabrielle's thorough understanding of the scene of Janus guarding his cherry tree. This form of reader response is intuitive for many children, and they love having permission to take out their drawing supplies. Therefore, *representational drawing* is one of the first strategies we teach, and students quickly make it their own.

In addition to envisioning the text, students often pick up on specific use of vocabulary as they label their drawings. For example, consider the representational drawing in Figure 13 of the barn in *Charlotte's Web* (White, 1952). Lauren Heinz and I watched as Henry, a fourth-grade ELL student, repeatedly went back into the book to revise and fill in details in his drawing, including the spelling of words. His labels include farm tools such as *rake, pick, shovel, wrench, scythe, ladder,* and a depiction of *haystacks.* His use of labels shows his understanding of these words. He also expresses a wonderful sense of humor that captures E. B. White's own playful, anthropomorphic tone. He shows the horse in a shower stall declaring, "I'm taking a shower," and the pigs in the pigpen "playing poker." One pig announces, "I got 7 sevens," another pig exclaims,

FIGURE 13. Henry's representational drawing of the barn in *Charlotte's Web*.

"No!," and a third pig says, "Get me out." His placement of animals and objects for three levels of the barn illustrates his active envisioning of life in the barn, which is such a central setting in the book.

Parking Lots

Parking lot is a strategy that fifth-grade teacher Lesley Doff taught us. It's a note-taking strategy for keeping running thoughts on and impressions of a text. Each year Lesley's students use this strategy often as they work their way through longer books that take days or perhaps weeks to finish. It becomes a useful strategy for introspective journeys through a book. After writing down the book title and date, Lesley teaches students what might be included in their parking lots: key words and phrases, "I wonder . . ." statements, questions, inferences, Wow! facts, key plot points, names and dates, quotes, reactions. The parking lot turns into sequential notes that provide a resource for retelling and holding on to important ideas in the book. Figure 14 is an example of one student's parking lot notes for *Wonder* (Palacio, 2012).

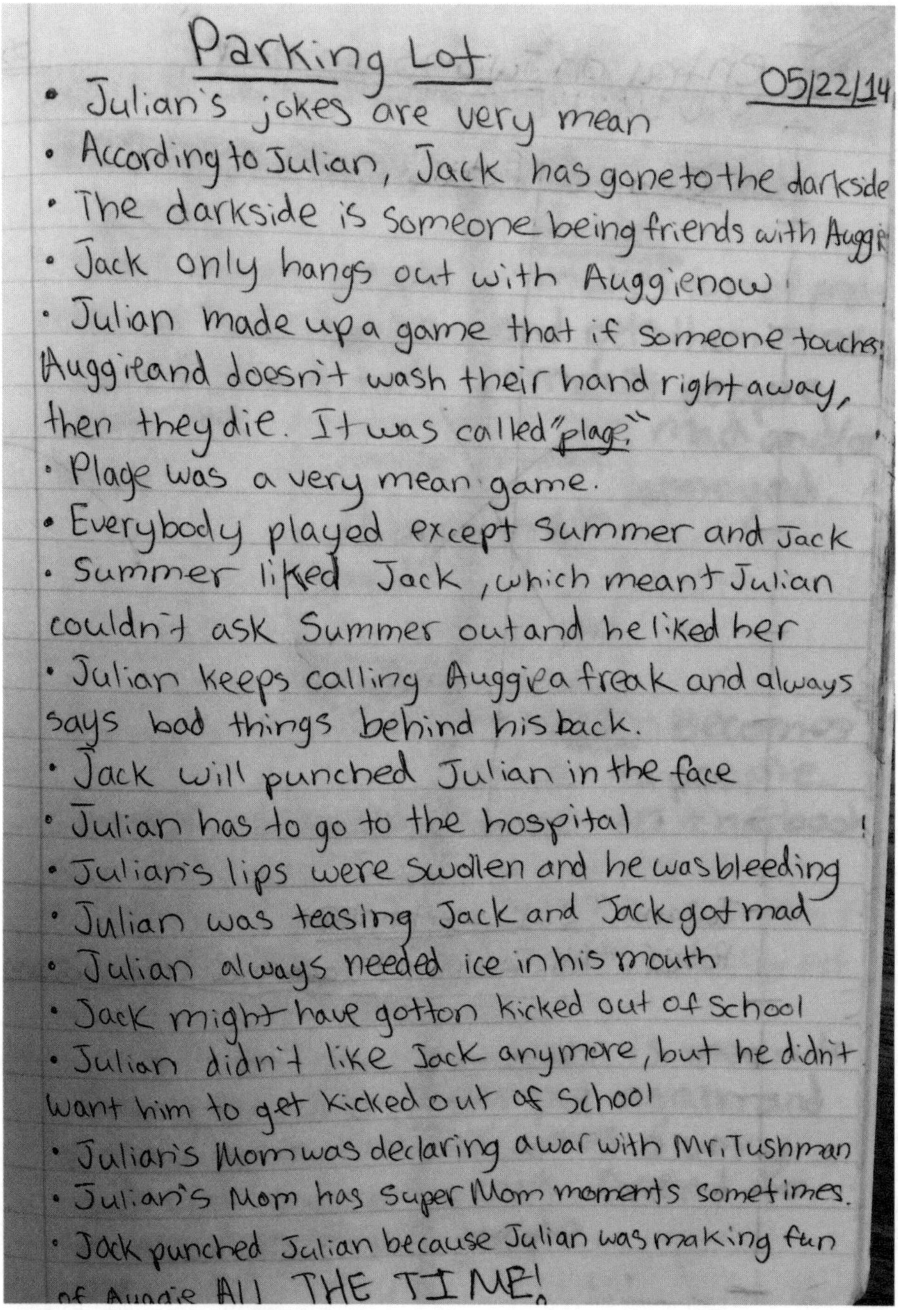

Parking Lot

05/22/14

- Julian's jokes are very mean
- According to Julian, Jack has gone to the darkside
- The darkside is someone being friends with Auggie
- Jack only hangs out with Auggie now
- Julian made up a game that if someone touches Auggie and doesn't wash their hand right away, then they die. It was called "plage"
- Plage was a very mean game.
- Everybody played except Summer and Jack
- Summer liked Jack, which meant Julian couldn't ask Summer out and he liked her
- Julian keeps calling Auggie a freak and always says bad things behind his back.
- Jack will punched Julian in the face
- Julian has to go to the hospital
- Julian's lips were swollen and he was bleeding
- Julian was teasing Jack and Jack got mad
- Julian always needed ice in his mouth
- Jack might have gotton kicked out of school
- Julian didn't like Jack anymore, but he didn't want him to get kicked out of school
- Julian's Mom was declaring a war with Mr. Tushman
- Julian's Mom has super Mom moments sometimes.
- Jack punched Julian because Julian was making fun of Auggie ALL THE TIME!

FIGURE 14. Parking lot for *Wonder*.

Summary Boxes and Essence Charts

Summary boxes and *essence charts* are two graphic organizers suggested by Fountas and Pinnell (2001) that we also use as introductory reading responses, especially when most children are reading fiction or nonfiction chapter books. These are both excellent strategies for summarizing or synthesizing each chapter, supporting recall of the plot and other information before the reader moves on in the book. In summary boxes, students write a few sentences that summarize what they believe are key plot points or important information in the chapter. In an essence chart, students write their takeaway, or what they consider to be the most essential occurrence or realization from each chapter.

As depicted in Phase 1 of Figure 11, we often demonstrate the use of these charts with chapter book read-alouds on large chart paper. After reading a chapter, I distribute one or two 3" × 5" sticky notes (depending on how much happened in that chapter) to each pair of students. I say, "Turn and talk to your partner; then, using your sticky note, write a summary of what we just read." I crouch down, listen in, and coach partnerships to write succinct summaries. We then share some of their responses. Next, we do a shared writing for proportionally sized summary boxes on the class chart. Students have the choice of copying what they wrote on their sticky notes or what we wrote on the class chart into their own RRNs for the whole-class read-aloud text. The class chart becomes a great resource for recalling what's happened in the book so far before starting the next chapter. Moreover, we sometimes collect their sticky note summaries as formative assessment. In these instances, we have each student write his or her own sticky note summary. As we read their summaries, we consider:

- Who is identifying important events or information in the chapter?
- Who is writing sequentially?
- Who is including names of characters, dates, places, and other important details?
- Who is showing awareness of setting?
- Who is using specific language from the text?

We are then able to share qualities of exemplary summaries to raise the level of writing summaries by all students. Once students get the hang of it, we transition them to Phase 2 of Figure 11: in conferences during independent reading time, we guide them in making summary boxes for the chapter books (both fiction and nonfiction) they are reading.

Deb Kessler's fourth-grade class was reading *Our Strange New Land: Elizabeth's Jamestown Colony Diary* (Hermes, 2002) for their study of Colonial America. It made sense for her students to keep summary boxes both to monitor their understanding and to support their small-group work. After all, they would need to build lots of background information in preparation for moving into their inquiry projects about Colonial America. Their summary boxes matched the diary structure of the book and helped students keep track of key events across time. Deb directed small groups to begin with their summaries before delving into their discussion questions. Figure 15 shows one page of one student's summary boxes.

English language learners of all ages have found these charts particularly supportive. One of my graduate students, Ji Young, who came from Korea in 2006 with only minimal English, found the use of summary boxes especially supportive as she prepared for her book club discussions of *The Watsons Go to Birmingham—1963* (Curtis, 1995). She explained that the process of writing each summary box pushed her to review each chapter and find the words she needed to get to "the heart of the action." Book club discussions often flowed too fast for Ji Young to join in. The summary boxes, however, provided a way to "have something to share with my group members."

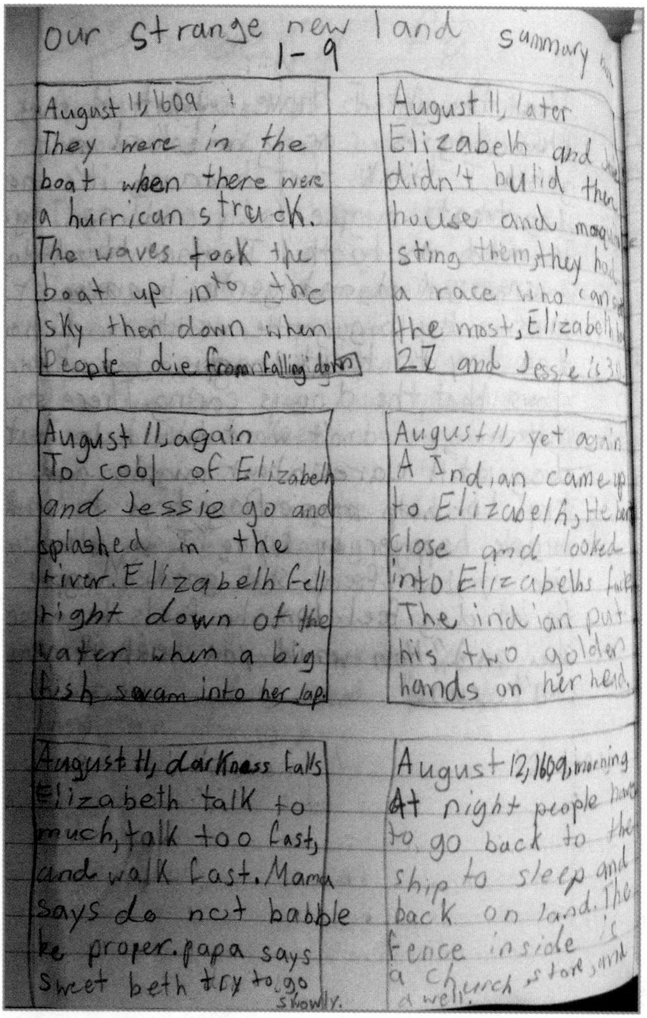

Some students who prefer the visual mode have created summary boxes in the form of comics. Figure 16a is an example by Natalie, a third grader, for the book *The Wretched Stone* (Van Allsburg, 1991), and Figure 16b is an example from Alyssa, a fifth grader, depicting a pivotal scene in *The Graduation of Jake Moon* (Park,

FIGURE 15. Summary boxes for *Our Strange New Land.*

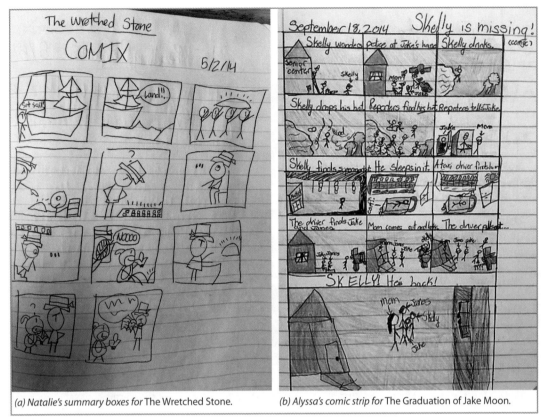

(a) Natalie's summary boxes for The Wretched Stone. (b) Alyssa's comic strip for The Graduation of Jake Moon.

FIGURE 16. Sample student summary boxes.

2002). Both examples illustrate how students co-opted a popular culture format for academic purposes, or what Dyson (2003b) calls "recontextualization": both students appropriated and reframed the use of comics for their own playful and productive purposes that converged with school-based literacy practices. This was possible only because their classroom teachers allowed it and recognized that this was yet another valid way to show their understanding.

In essence charts, students write what they consider most important for each chapter or section of the book. Essence charts work particularly well for nonfiction texts. Figure 17 is an example of a fourth grader's use of an essence chart for a nonfiction chapter book about sea turtles. Ella includes names of sea turtles that are discussed and some "Wow!" facts. After learning the literary term *parody* in Lesley Doff's fifth-grade class, Rachel drew the following "parody" for the Narnia series by distilling the basic structure of each book (see Figure 18). She also parodied the formal English in the series by having the children use text talk and modern English, such as YOLO (You Only Live Once), WOAN (not sure), and "That was an awesome time!" Rachel doesn't need to be tested on a

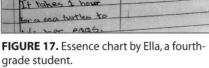

FIGURE 17. Essence chart by Ella, a fourth-grade student.

FIGURE 18. A parody of the Narnia series.

definition of parody. Instead, using simple line drawings in a flow map, she gets to the structural essence of these books in a comical way.

Figure 19 consists of summary boxes that fifth grader Evan wrote for *The Bully Book* (Gale, 2013) that function like an essence chart. He summarizes each major plot development in the left-hand column, and then elaborates on why this matters in the right-hand column. Notice how he uses all capital letters and exclamation marks to summarize later chapters as the tension in the mystery mounts. Across these examples, we see how inventive students can become with this strategy to keep track of their thinking, enhancing their introspective journeys through books.

Lifelong Lists

One more starting structure that we introduce to students is keeping *lifelong lists* in the back of their RRNs. Lifelong lists are ongoing lists to keep track of activities and topics that readers care about. I share with students lifelong lists that I keep: movies I want to see, books I want to read, favorite movies, songs

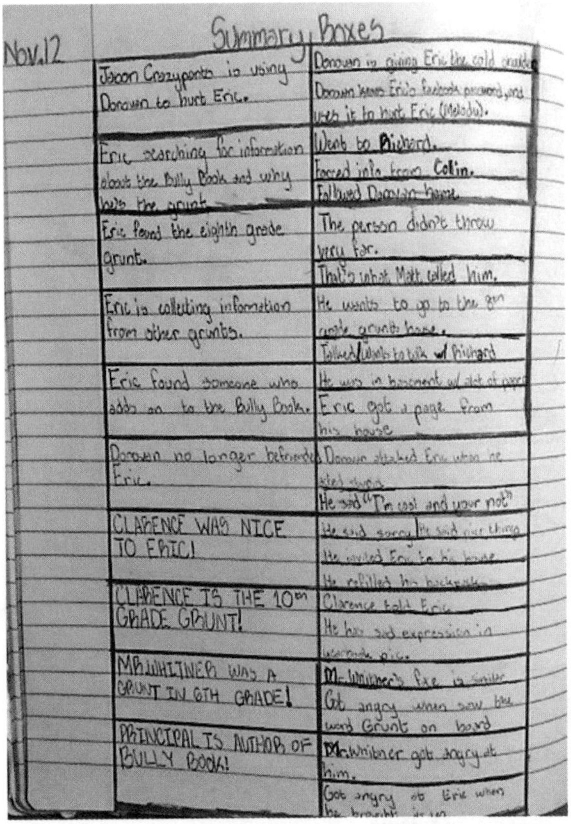

FIGURE 19. A blended summary box and essence chart.

I want to learn on guitar or violin, places in the world I want to visit, favorite restaurants, etc. We then guide students to name one to three lists they want to start in the back of their notebooks. They count ten pages in from the end and mark that page with a sticky note to indicate the start of their lifelong lists. We instruct them to give each list a title and to use a sticky note or fold a page over as a tab for each list. We then give them time in class to start their lists. Some students migrate toward the class library for book titles. Then, after twenty minutes of listing and laughing at some of their lists and items on their lists, students share in small groups, generating even more ideas for lists they might keep. We hear comments such as: "I didn't know you like Star Trek movies. Me, too!" "Oh. I've been to DR [the Dominican Republic] also." "You just gave me an idea to list my favorite football teams." Students are discovering common and new interests and building community.

We remind students throughout the year to add to their lists and generate new ones. Before the end of reading time, for example, the teacher announces: "Please take ten minutes now to read through and add to your lifelong lists. I'll then signal you to share with your partner." Or, when a teacher notices that one student has a particular obsession, perhaps Major League baseball, she might prompt him: "How about keeping a list of your all-time favorite players, their positions, and the years they played?" Figure 20 offers examples of students' lists. In Figure 20a, Nikola lists topics she's interested in. She was a newly arrived immigrant, so notice how one of her topics is "how to get friends in public school in my class." Notice how fourth grader Wissal, in Figure 20b, uses color coding to further distinguish her categories for "Favorite Movies."

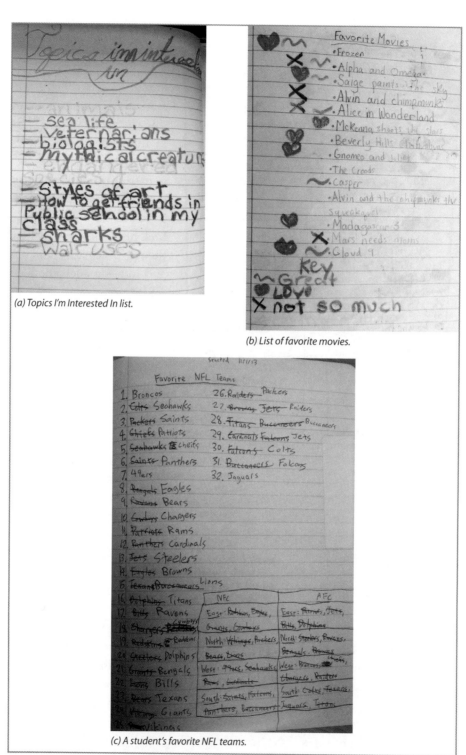

(a) Topics I'm Interested In list.

(b) List of favorite movies.

(c) A student's favorite NFL teams.

FIGURE 20. Examples of students' lifelong lists.

POSSIBLE LIFELONG LISTS	
• Favorite books	• Favorite quotes
• Books I want to read next	• Series I love
• Favorite movies	• Favorite video games
• Movies I want to see	• Favorite book characters
• Favorite TV shows	• Topics I want to learn about
• Songs I love	• Places I love to visit
• Texting terms	• Favorite foods
• Favorite restaurants	• Favorite flowers
• Places in the world I want to visit	• Concerns about the world
• Words I love	• Cool digital tools
• Words I hate	• Favorite roller coasters
• Favorite apps	• What I'm thankful for

FIGURE 21. Potential topics for ongoing lists.

In Figure 20c, fifth grader Michael indicates on top when he started this list of favorite NFL teams. His embedded chart of NFC and AFC teams helps him account for all teams, and as the season unfolds, he makes revisions to his list.

Through sharing in each classroom community, we create a chart of "Possible Lifelong Lists" as a reference. Figure 21 shows one example of this chart. How does keeping these ongoing lists support leading a literate life? First, these lists get students in the habit of paying attention to their world. Literate people are interested in the world around them. This is a starting point for engagement. Second, these lists propel students to pay attention to language. Consider the language that students are gathering when they keep lists of favorite texting terms or "Words I Love" or "Words I Hate." Readers and writers are wordsmiths; keeping these lists is a start on that journey. Third, these lists build community. When students share these lists, they discover common interests, they learn and support one another's interests, and they get new ideas. Fourth, these lists generate reading and writing interests. In addition to "Books I Want to Read," consider a list such as "Places in the World I Want to Visit." What reading and writing work might a student do to develop these agendas? Fifth, these lists inform our work as teachers. For the same list of "Places in the World I Want to Visit," how might I, as this student's teacher, support this agenda in our classroom community? How might this interest connect with curriculum work we are doing? What revisions to the curriculum might I make by keeping this interest in mind? Ultimately, these lists support students in building permeable boundaries between who they are outside of school and who they can be in the classroom (Dyson, 2003b). Discovering their identities in literate behaviors is a powerful source for building literate lives.

In Chapter 3, I continue with more starting strategies for the RRN, building a repertoire, with the use of an anchor chart, toward agency, autonomy, and accountability.

Strategies for Carving Out Time for Responding in Notebooks

A typical response takes fifteen minutes, depending on the response strategy a student is using. How do we find time in our busy daily schedule for RRN work? RRN work becomes more fluid and integrated into classroom life as the school year progresses, just as writer's notebooks do. As students gain more agency and autonomy (Phase 3 of Figure 11), they learn how to manage their responses on their own. Like most tools and routines, RRN work takes most time in the first months of the school year (Phases 1 and 2 of Figure 11). This time is worth it because gradual release of responsibility leads to students' agency and autonomy. Here are strategies to help you carve out time for this work in each phase of the process.

Phase 1: Whole Class	Phase 2: Guided Work	Phase 3: Independent Reading/ Partnerships/Reading Clubs
• Whole-class text • Demonstration of strategy • Strategy: Try it for another part of the text, alone or in partnerships • Share (Chapter 2 and 3)	• Whole-class strategy • Demonstration of strategy • Strategy: Try it for independent reading • Share (Chapter 2 and 3)	• Strategy of choice • Text of choice • Share (Chapters 4 and 5)
• Two to three times per week, extend interactive read-aloud to an entire period (45 min.). Have interactive read-aloud (15 min.), teach a strategy (10 min.), have students practice their responses using this strategy (15 min.), share (5 min.). After introducing each new strategy, add it to a class anchor chart (see Table 1). • Make some starting strategies the focus of an entire reading workshop session (45 min.), such as when you explore what a text is, introducing reading logs, or when you first introduce ongoing lists. Each week in the first month of school, reserve two reading workshop sessions for this work.	• After introducing new strategies on the anchor chart, make each strategy the focus of a minilesson at the start of reading workshop time (45 min.) so students can now apply the strategy to their independent reading. With 20 minutes remaining, remind students to practice the strategy in their notebooks (if they have not yet done so). Reserve the final 10 minutes to share their responses with a partner or small group. • Actively confer about students' use of strategies on the anchor chart. (See Chapter 4 for examples of conferences.)	• If you are consistent, within two to three months you and your students will generate more strategies than you can list on the anchor chart (see Chapters 4 and 5). Teach more mini-lessons at the start of reading workshop that demonstrate choice and purpose for reader response (agency). • Set the expectation of three entries per week during independent reading time. Entries first happen in school, but once you and your students establish routines, entries might also happen at home. • Provide students with "Readers Notebook Strategies" checklist (see Appendix A; Chapter 4) to keep track of strategies they are using. • Grade students' RRN work using the "Notebook Checklist" (see Appendix B; Chapter 4). If you grade their notebooks consistently (once every two weeks) with feedback, students will learn to take this work seriously.

Expanding Possibilities

I n Chapter 2, I explained some processes and activities for getting started
with the new vision of the reader response notebook that this book presents,
applying Phases 1 and 2 of Figure 11. In this chapter, I take you into classrooms to experience more strategies and the supports we provide so that students use these strategies purposefully and creatively. I explain how we guide
students toward more independence, or Phase 3 of Figure 11. By expanding students' use of the RRN, I prepare them for the focus of Chapter 4, toward agency,
autonomy, and accountability.

More "Getting Started" Strategies

In every class I work with, each strategy we introduce is added to an anchor
chart that names the strategy, describes how to use the strategy, and provides
some purposes of the strategy (see Table 1). Some of the early-in-the-year strategies we teach include sketch-to-stretch, representational drawing, parking lot,
summary boxes and essence charts, ongoing lists (all explained in Chapter 2),
character lists, character webs of relationships, found poetry, and reformulations
(this chapter). Appendix C is a complete RRN strategy chart for twenty-eight
strategies we have taught elementary school students to use. As students invent
new strategies (see Chapter 5), these also become part of the anchor chart. Some
classes even name the strategy after the student who invented it: e.g., "Emily's
strategy."

Character Lists

For texts with many characters, such as some TV series and movies, as well as
some novels, histories, and biographies, keeping a *character list* supports comprehension. A list helps students to retell, summarize, synthesize, and infer character relationships. Consider all the characters that populate the Harry Potter
series, for example. A character list would certainly help to keep them straight in

TABLE 1. RNN Strategy Chart

RRN Strategy Chart		
Strategy	**What**	**Why**
Sketch-to-Stretch	Make a sketch using colors, lines, shapes, symbols. Write a title and a caption that explains your sketch.	• To explore character relationships or qualities of a character • To explore conflicts in a story • To explore how setting influences characters
Representational Drawing	Make a sketch or drawing using colors, as if you were hired as the illustrator of the text. Rely on details in the text. Write a title and a caption that explain your drawing.	• To envision the setting • To envision an important object or character or event that is carefully described in the text
Parking Lot	Jot down notes and impressions as you read or listen to or view the text. You might record buzz-words, key phrases, predictions, wonderings, key plot developments, new information, a quote. Use bullets or numbered statements. Write shorthand.	• To record your impressions of the text in the process of reading it • To review your impressions to gain new insights and develop theories about the text
Summary Boxes	After each section or chapter of a text, summarize it in one or two of the boxes in the chart.	• To remember what you've read so far, especially if it takes a few days to finish the text
Essence Chart	After each section or chapter of a text, write what you think is the most important, interesting, or essential part.	• To pay attention to new or surprising or compelling parts of a story or biography or informational text
List of Characters	Keep an ongoing list of characters. You might use symbols to indicate central or secondary characters, or animals, or Muggles, or children, or evil characters, etc.	• To sort out and keep track of characters in a story, especially when there are lots of them (e.g., the Harry Potter books or a favorite TV series)
Character Web of Relationships	Create a web of characters' names. Use colors, lines, shapes, spacing, special fonts, and other symbols to show the connections between characters. Be sure to include a key or legend that explains your use of colors, lines, and other symbols.	• To show the relationships among characters
Found Poetry	Create a poem using key phrases from a text and poetry elements, such as repetition, line breaks, stanzas, a refrain, a title. While you can put phrases in any sequence, you are not allowed to alter the words.	• To develop an aesthetic appreciation for the craft of writing in the text • To use poetic elements to express the essence of a text
Reformulations	Use other forms or genres to reformulate the content of a text. For example, you might use a flow map to show a process; a chart to show different categories of animals; a diagram to show a living thing; a graph to show a growth cycle; a poem to appreciate beautiful language.	• To think more about information in a text • To represent information in a new way • To use creativity to imagine new possibilities for a text

a reader's mind. Applying Phase 2 of Figure 11, we demonstrate using the exact spelling of each character's name for written texts and forming the list down the page. We also clue students in to notice nicknames, last names, and other references to each character, teaching them to use the acronym aka for "also known as." We then guide students to code their lists for their independent reading books or for any meaningful text in their lives. For example, which characters are main characters? Perhaps mark them with an asterisk (*). Which characters are wizards and which are Muggles? Which characters are adults, which are children, which are animals? The coding students choose is particular to the text they are responding to. Students' choices of drawing materials and color might also carry meaning for how they list and code the characters.

We smile in appreciation as we observe students going back into their texts for accurate retrieval of details. Did the text provide the character's last name? How come her last name is different from her dad's? Does the story refer to the boy only as *boy*? Why would the author not give a name to the character? Did you know that the scientific name for desert cactuses is *saguaro* and that you say *cacti*, NOT *cactuses*? These are comments we overhear as students explore in their own texts, and we pick up on these comments to guide our conferences. This is one form of close reading that is strongly expected in state and national ELA standards.

Figure 22 highlights examples of four students' character lists, which collectively demonstrate students' expanded conceptions of what counts as a text, as well as their attention to character roles and relationships, nicknames, and conventions of language. For example, their lists show evidence of the use of titles, quotations, parentheses, brackets, commas, correct spelling of characters' names, dashes, 's for possessives, and capitalization. For *Scat* (Hiaasen, 2009; Figure 22a), fourth grader Dyandra coded for main, secondary, and background characters, and whether they were good or bad. Meanwhile, fourth grader Vicky made a character list for *Ben Franklin's Almanac* (Fleming, 2003; Figure 22b), a nonfiction text the class was studying in social studies. She created a key demarcating political positions and traits (from an American perspective) of central characters. Vicky used green tape to draw attention to her two text boxes and give her entry the feel of a scrapbook. In Figure 22c, notice the extensive details that fifth grader Michael provides in his character list for *The Big Bang Theory*. In Figure 22d, fourth grader Andrew presented similar depth of analysis for his favorite soccer team, Bayern Munich. These lists are a testament to the depth of thinking young readers can achieve for any text they engage with purposefully, including popular culture texts.

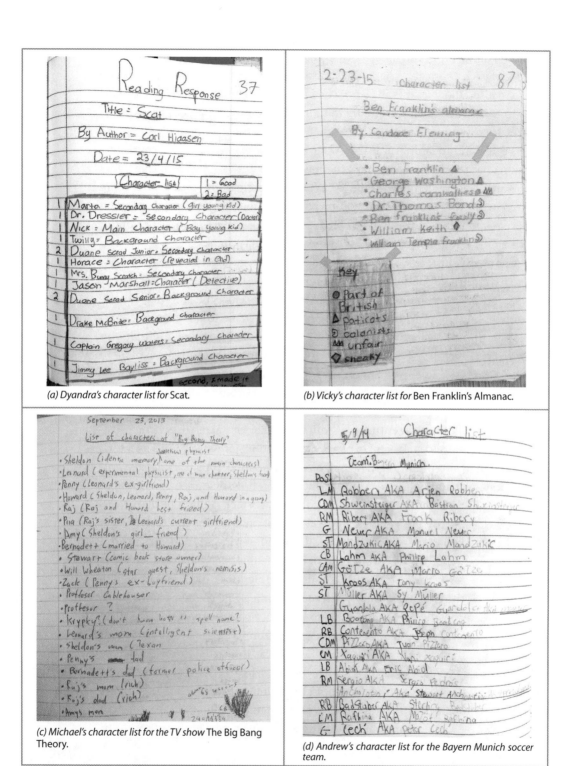

(a) Dyandra's character list for Scat.

(b) Vicky's character list for Ben Franklin's Almanac.

(c) Michael's character list for the TV show The Big Bang Theory.

(d) Andrew's character list for the Bayern Munich soccer team.

FIGURE 22. Examples of students' character lists.

Character Web of Relationships

Students quickly gain proficiency with character lists. The proof: they create character lists for texts they love, such as *The Big Bang Theory*. A week later, we teach students how to create a *character web of relationships*. In this strategy, students use layout, arrows, color, size, shapes, fonts, and other design features to show the characters in relationship to one another. We also model how to include a key or legend to explain their design choices.

I'm sitting next to the whiteboard easel in front of Lauren Heinz's fourth-grade class. Twenty-eight students sit on the carpet facing me.

"You know how we created a character list for *Tiger Rising* [DiCamillo, 2006] last week?" This was the whole-class read-aloud, so all the students knew the book well. Students nod as I show them the list of characters with symbols and colors. "What's some of the information this list gives us?" I ask. "Turn and tell your partner." I listen in as students share the names of characters, other ways they are referred to in the story, who is a main character and who a secondary character, who is a grown-up and who a child, why the tiger is included on the list. After two minutes, I call the students back to attention. "Wow! So this list definitely gives us lots of useful information. But what a list doesn't show is the relationships between characters. After all, we know that one of the best parts of a story is how characters interact with each other. For example, what's the relationship like between Rob Horton and his dad, Robert Horton? They love each other, but they have a lot of pain and silence between them. How do they both feel about Rob's mom, Caroline Horton?" Students are now nodding and interjecting, showing their understanding. "Hmm, how would we show these interactions? One way is by drawing what I call 'a character web of relationships.' To make it, we use colors and characters' names and arrows and circles to show their relationships."

Now I start drawing on the whiteboard. "I think I'll start with Rob Horton, since the book is mostly focused on him." I write his name in the middle and circle it. "Now, he definitely has a complicated relationship with his dad." I write Robert Horton's name above Rob's name and circle it. "I'm gonna write *Robert Horton* here, above Rob's name, to show that he's the dad and Rob depends on him. They love each other, but they also have a lot of pain between them." I pick up the red dry erase marker and draw a thick, dashed double-headed arrow as I say, "I'm making the arrow thick to show that they have strong love for each other, but also I'm using dashes to show that their relationship has a lot of pain." Looking back at our list, I say, "Then there's Rob's mom, Caroline Horton. Where should we write her name?"

"How about on the side between Rob and his dad," Lilian says, "because they both miss her so much."

As I write Caroline's name and circle it, I ask, "What kind of arrow should I draw now? Should I use a red marker to show love?"

"I think you should use blue," Marcos suggests. "Like, we say, 'I'm feeling blue,' when we're sad."

"Ooh, I like that suggestion," I respond. "What kinda arrow? Turn and tell your partner." I crouch and listen in. After a minute, I call students back together and call on Andrew.

"A thick blue arrow from the dad to the mom and from Rob to the mom."

"A double-headed arrow?" I ask.

"No. One way. They both miss her a lot and definitely feel blue."

We move on. I next write Sistine Bailey's name. The students suggest writing her name next to Rob's name, and I circle it.

"Don't draw it red," Angela calls out. "They don't love each other," and other kids chuckle. "They have a strong friendship."

"Make it a two-way arrow in green," Michaela says, and I draw this arrow.

"What about Sistine and Rob's dad?" I ask, pointing to the two names on our emerging web. After another turn and talk, we decide that Sistine feels bad for Rob's dad, and they sorta like each other. We decide to represent this relationship with a thin orange line. For the next few minutes, we keep building our web. I write "Web of Relationships for *The Tiger Rising*" and underline the heading. On the bottom right corner, I write a key box using a small color square and indicate the meaning of each color.

"I would like each of you to make your own character web for *The Tiger Rising*. Look at your character list in your notebook. Then on a new page, begin making your web." I send students off to work at their tables, where they work, share, and discuss their webs. Figures 23 is an example of this work.

In the next few days, as we conferred with students, they quickly transferred this strategy to their independent reading books (Phase 2 of our gradual release of responsibility model, Figure 11). Students produced some particularly interesting examples when we asked a guided reading group in Lauren Heinz's fourth grade to respond to *Those*

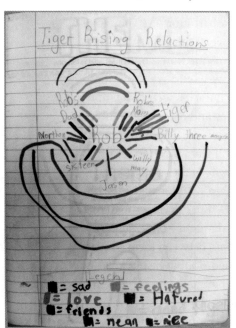

FIGURE 23. Character web of relationships for *The Tiger Rising*.

Shoes (Boelts & Jones, 2007). Notice the distinctiveness of two students' responses in Figures 24a and b, showing the versatility of this strategy. Meanwhile, Vicky, in Deb Kessler's class, converted her character list for *Ben Franklin's Almanac* (Fleming, 2003; Figure 22b) into a character web of relationships (Figure 24c). By inventing codes and using colors, lines, placement on the page, and different

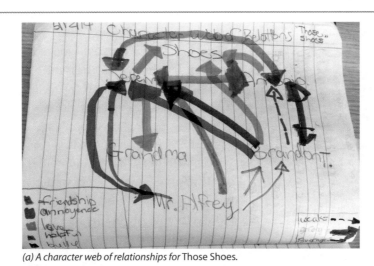

(a) A character web of relationships for Those Shoes.

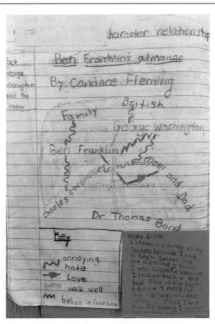

(b) A character web of relationships for Those Shoes.

(c) A character web of relationships for Ben Franklin's Almanac.

FIGURE 24. Examples of character webs of relationships.

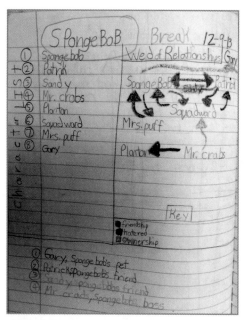

FIGURE 25. Miguel's character web of relationships for *Sponge Bob Square Pants.*

fonts—in other words, by applying design elements—students revealed deep inferential thinking about character relationships in the diverse texts they read. Students were also proud of these responses. When we had them choose and write sticky note reflections on their favorite entries, Vicky chose this entry, twice! She was proud of the symbols she used in her key and declared that she was "successful because I looked back in the book." She felt this was her best entry because she really considered the characters' feelings.

As students gained proficiency with this strategy, they also started applying it to popular culture texts, blending school-based literacy practices with texts that mattered in their lives—again, building permeable boundaries between home and school (Dyson, 2003b). This is a topic I address thoroughly in Chapter 5. Students were now implementing Phase 3 of Figure 11. Figure 25 is an example from Laura Heinz's fourth graders for the TV show *Sponge Bob Square Pants.* Students were asked to respond to a text they had read during Thanksgiving break. Miguel applied the same deep analytical thinking appropriate for any school-based text, using both a character list on the left side of the page, with more details at the bottom, and a character web of relationships on the right side of the page, along with a key to explain his symbols.

Found Poems

Found poetry is a well-established form of poetry. Wikipedia provides the following straightforward definition:

> Found poetry is a type of poetry created by taking words, phrases, and sometimes whole passages from other sources and reframing them as poetry (a literary equivalent of a collage) by making changes in spacing and lines, or by adding or deleting text, thus imparting new meaning. (https://en.wikipedia.org/wiki/Found_poetry).

Because the words and phrases are already determined, once students have derived key messages from the text, they can focus on the craft of writing, applying other poetic elements that will enhance the meanings they arrive at.

It helps if students already have some poetic elements in their writing toolkits, such as repetition, pattern, line breaks, stanzas, special fonts, alliteration, and titles, to support their creation of found poems. As a classroom teacher, I provided this awareness by making poetry part of our weekly shared reading experience. I introduced three poems a week, on chart paper, in Big Books, or projected on the screen, that we read daily as a warm-up to other activities. Then, on Fridays, my students received a copy of the three poems on one page that they placed in their poetry binder. Their homework was to illustrate the poems and practice reading them aloud by sharing them with family members. Figure 26 is one example from Luiko, one of my more artistic third-grade

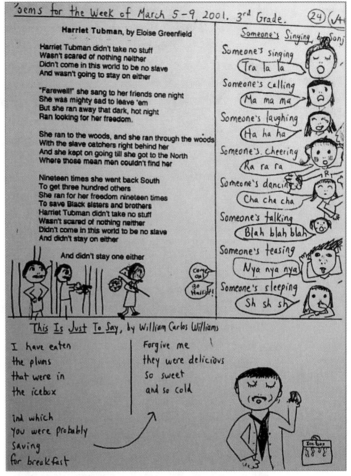

FIGURE 26. Illustrated poems by a third-grade student.

students. As my students accumulated a wide array of poems, cumulatively they developed an awareness of the poetic elements that poets use.

As in most fourth-grade classrooms, Lauren Heinz's students had read *Charlotte's Web* (White, 1952). One morning I provide copies of a passage at the start of Chapter 3 that describes the barn. This is an excellent choice for practicing found poetry because the passage is only two paragraphs long and is beautifully crafted: parallel phrases, patterns, repetition, alliteration, lists of precise nouns, sensory details, and rhythm. The writing is strongly structured, with the first paragraph focusing entirely on barn smells. In other words, the passage has so many embedded poetic elements that it provides a perfect practice text for writing found poems. Even if the students hadn't been familiar with this book or hadn't seen the animated movie, the passage is strong enough to stand on its own.

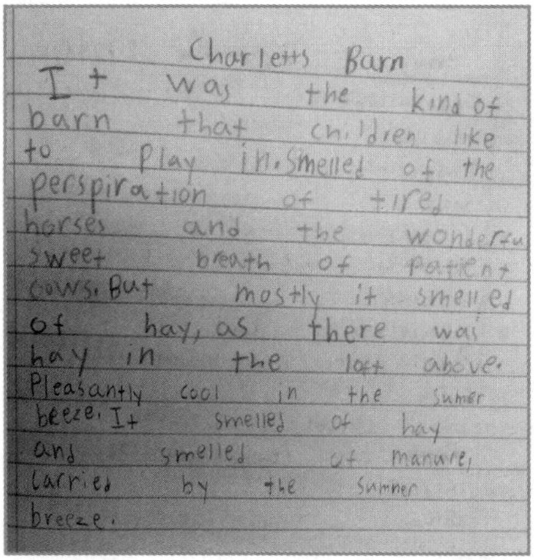
Charletts Barn
It was the kind of
barn that children like
to Play in. Smelled of the
perspiration of tired
horses and the wonderfu
sweet breath of patient
cows. But mostly it smelled
of hay, as there was
hay in the loft above.
Pleasantly cool in the sumer
beeze. It smelled of hay
and smelled of manure,
carried by the summer
breeze.

FIGURE 27. A found poem from *Charlotte's Web.*

After reading the passage aloud, I tell the students to underline words and phrases that stood out to them, that they think are beautiful or create a strong image for them: "you can picture it in your head or you just think it's beautiful." Lauren and I circulate, conferring with students as they read closely. After a few minutes, we reconvene.

"Today, we're going to write found poems." After providing a definition, I say, "Here are the rules. You can repeat phrases or change the order of phrases, but you cannot change any of the words that E. B. White used." I display one of the poems the class has used for shared reading to remind the students of line breaks and stanzas and a title. Then students get to work. Figure 27 is an example of one student's response. True, this student could now benefit from the use of line breaks and stanzas. But also notice how many poetic elements the student applied. She shortened phrases, applying the distilled brevity of poetry. She applied repetition and parallel phrases. She chose beautiful language and adapted White's sentence complexity and variety for lyrical rhythm. Moreover, the process enabled her to apply correct conventions of language and sophisticated vocabulary, such as "the perspiration of tired horses."

The teachers and students delighted in these creative responses, and in subsequent sessions we applied found poetry to nonfiction texts they were reading in social studies, moving the strategy from Phase 1 to Phase 2 of Figure 11. Meantime, their responses showed us which poetic elements they applied and which ones they needed additional instruction in, such as line breaks, stanzas, special fonts, and poignant endings. In social studies, for example, Deb Kessler's class was studying Colonial America. After reading a chapter about the rise of the free press, Deb told students to list key words and phrases and then create their found poem. Figure 28 is one student's result. By applying poetic elements such as phrasing and line breaks, this response is more than a summary. Aurellia applies elements of style, with heightened attention to language to create a compelling account.

Reformulations

Before I visited Lauren Heinz's fourth-grade class one fall day, Lauren had read aloud *Cactus Hotel* (Guiberson & Lloyd, 1991). This nonfiction book teaches about the giant saguaro cacti in the Sonoran Desert. The morning I came in, I

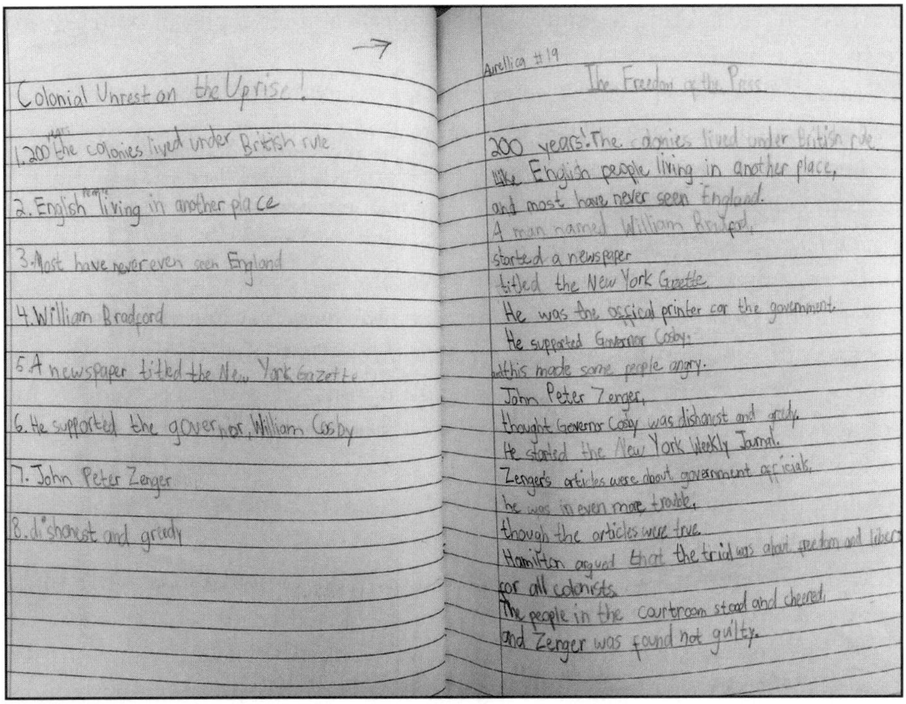

FIGURE 28. A found poem about Colonial America.

read aloud *Desert Giant: The World of the Saguaro Cactus* (Bash, 1989). Focusing on the same topic, the books have both overlapping and distinct information. We provided typed copies of both texts so students could look back for text evidence as they worked on their responses.

On the day of my visit, I wanted to introduce students to *reformulations* (Beers, 2003; Dorn & Soffos, 2005; Feathers, 1993). In this response strategy, readers reformulate a text they read into a new visual display that the text itself didn't provide. For example, they might create a chart to support character analysis, or a diagram to depict the structure of a heart, or a web to explore all the forces at play in the American Revolution. Reformulations harness students' creativity, encourage them to do close readings to meet the purposes of their reformulations, deepen their grasp of structural elements of the original text, and propel students to develop new insights about textual concepts. I wanted to provide students with some choices in how they might reformulate the information in these two books about saguaro cacti.

After finishing *Desert Giant*, the students return to their work spaces. I hold up both books and tell students to take out both of their typewritten texts. "So what did you notice was the same or different in these two books?" I ask.

Tony states, "*Desert Giant* tells us about the Tohono O'odham Indians. *Cactus*

Hotel doesn't even bring them up." Students look at their copies of both texts to verify that what Tony said is true.

Amanda then says, "Well, *Cactus Hotel* shows us the life of one cactus, from seed to when it dies. *Desert Giant* talks more about all the saguaro cactus."

Lesley adds, "Yeah, *Desert Giant* tells us about the Sonoran Desert, and that's not brought up at all in *Cactus Hotel*." Again, the students take a look in their copied texts to see if this is true.

By engaging in this comparison work, we are addressing most of the grade 4 state and national standards for informational text, such as describing similarities and differences in focus and information that both texts provide. We continue with this comparison for a few more minutes. The students notice, for example, that both books discuss some of the same birds, such as the woodpecker, the elf owl, and the Harris hawk. I then bring up the titles of both books. What do the authors mean by *Cactus Hotel* or *Desert Giant*? We first think about what a hotel is and what a giant is. "Hmm, what does a saguaro cactus have to do with a hotel or with a giant?" I ask. Students talk about this in their small groups before we share their thoughts as a class.

"So, we're noticing how no book can tell all information. One book will give more information about one focus, and another book will give you more information about something else. And we might wish that both books provided information that we still think is missing. That is where *reformulations* come in." I write the word on the board and then have students say the word, clap the word, and notice parts of the word. After explaining what reformulations are for reader response, I announce, "One kind of reformulation that would be useful to make is what the cactus hotel looks like when all the animals are living in it, both when the cactus is alive and when it's dead. We only get a partial view of the cactus hotel," and I show them those pages in *Cactus Hotel*. "I'll put both books here on display, but using your copies of both texts, take out your drawing supplies and show what the cactus hotel looked like when fully occupied."

Students open their RRNs and, with both texts out, get to work. Lauren and I confer and support students as they look for text evidence for their illustrations. They are now making decisions they hadn't even considered before. What animals live in the ground, or in the middle of the cactus? What animals live on top? Where are the flowers? Which animals live on the branches, or in the holes? What animals live in the dead cactus? We see students underlining details and returning to their illustrations, now selecting the right color crayons to depict the cactus and each kind of animal. Is the Harris hawk completely black? What color stripes does the snake have? What does the dead cactus look like? The students are engaging in close reading that again addresses state and national standards for informational text, especially integration of knowledge and ideas. Figures 29a and b are examples of the students' reformulations.

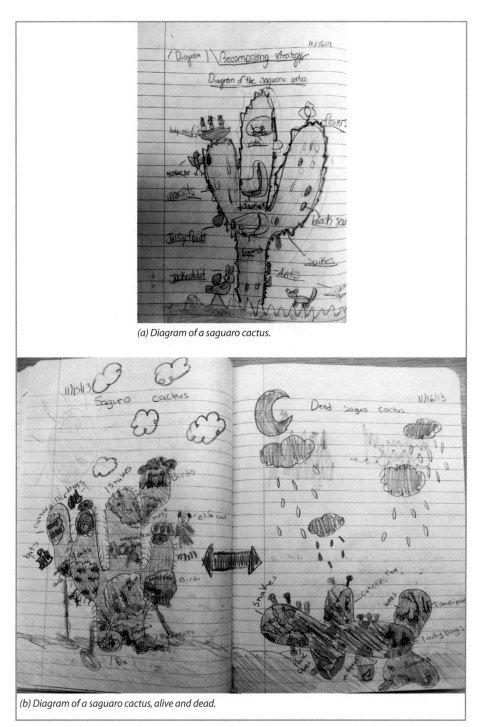

(a) Diagram of a saguaro cactus.

(b) Diagram of a saguaro cactus, alive and dead.

FIGURE 29. Student examples of reformulations.

On a subsequent day, I revisit *Cactus Hotel* and *Desert Giant* with the students. I hold up both books and say, "Last time, we worked on one reformulation of these two books. Remember? We drew what the cactus hotel might have looked like, alive and dead. Open up your reading response notebooks to your illustrations." I give them a minute to do this. "How did making these illustrations help you to learn about saguaro cactus?"

Jonathan says, "I had to think about all the animals that use the cactus, both when it's alive and dead."

Cynthia adds, "I had to think about where the animals lived in the cactus and what they looked like."

Patricia says, "I wasn't sure about some of the sizes of the animals."

"Ahh," I comment, "so we may need to look at other resources to find out. Where might we look?"

"You can Google it," I hear some students say.

"Yeah, we could. What would we type if we wanted to find out, let's say, the size of the Harris hawk?"

Kimberly responds, "'size of Harris Hawk'?"

"Yeah, that could definitely work." I was emphasizing being text users. According to Freebody and Luke (1990), literate people express four dimensions of literacy: they are **code breakers**, or people who know how to decode and encode print and other texts; they are **meaning makers**, or people who actively use strategies to make sense of the texts they read and write; they are **text users**, or people who know how to find and use texts as resources to get things done in the world; and they are **text critics**, or people who recognize inherent bias in texts and know how to challenge it.

"There are other ways of reformulating these texts; other ways of representing the information in these books. Today, let's think of some other reformulations. Hmm," I muse, as I scroll through *Cactus Hotel*, "we might think of the animals that actively participate in the life of the cactus before, during, and after it's alive, or I was wondering about which animals are awake during the day (diurnal) versus which animals are awake at night (nocturnal). How might we show that information?" I ask.

Brandon answers, "We could make a chart."

"Yeah. So, if we made a chart, how might it go? How would we set it up?" I ask. The students look uncertain, so I continue, "Well, I was thinking we could have two columns. In the first column, I would have the diurnal animals, and in the next column, the nocturnal animals," and I draw this on the whiteboard. "How about if we want to represent the animals before, during, and after the cactus is alive?" Now some hands go up.

Amy says, "You could have a row for before, a row for during, and a row for after," and I again draw this chart on the whiteboard as Amy speaks.

"I know that both texts talk about the animals, so you probably would use both texts to help you with that one. Any other reformulations you can think of?" I ask. I know the students are studying graphs in math, so I say, "Well, I was thinking of showing the growth of the cactus in its life span." I turn to *Cactus Hotel*. "I remember that *Cactus Hotel* kept telling us how big the cactus was at specific years," and now I turn the pages of the book. "Like here, it says, 'After ten years, the cactus is only four inches high.' Wow! Show me four inches with your fingers. That's not much growth for ten years." I continue turning the pages. "And here it says, 'After twenty-five years the cactus is two feet tall.' Show me two feet with your hands. That's still not much growth for twenty-five years. Oh, and here it says, 'After fifty years the cactus stands ten feet tall.' Wow! Now it's getting tall. That's as tall as a basketball hoop." I continue turning the pages. "Oh, and here it says, 'After sixty years the cactus hotel is eighteen feet tall.' I wonder how tall it gets. Anyone find that information?"

Jonathan calls out, "I found it!" He reads aloud, "After a hundred and fifty years, there are holes of every size in the cactus, too. The giant plant has finally stopped growing. It is fifty feet tall, with seven long branches."

"Wow! Fifty feet tall! Imagine that! That's way taller than the ceiling!" I exclaim. "So how would we represent the cactus's growth over time? I know you've been studying graphs and charts in math. Could we use a graph or chart?"

Beatrice says, "We could make a graph showing its height across years," and I again show the graph template as Beatrice speaks, with years on the x-axis and height in feet on the y-axis.

"Any other reformulations?" I ask. Again, students seem uncertain. "Well, I remember last time we noticed that only *Desert Giant* discusses the Tohono O'odham Indians. Anyone remember what the book showed about these people?"

The students turn to that part of the text and start rereading. A few hands go up.

Jonathan says, "It shows how they make jam and syrup and wine from the cactus fruit."

"So that's a process," I say. "When we think about a process, about how to do something, how might we show the steps?" I ask.

"A flow map," a few students call out.

I draw a blank flow map on the whiteboard and, looking at the pages in *Desert Giant*, I touch the first box: "First, they gather the fruit using long poles. Next," touching the second box, "they put the red fruit in a basket. Then," touching the third box, "they remove pebbles from the fruit pulp and get the fire ready. They mix the pulp with water and cook it for a long time," I say, touching the fourth box. "They pour it through a wire mesh to separate out the seeds," I say, as I touch the fifth box. Touching the sixth box, I say, "They use the fruit liquid to make syrup, candy, jams, and wine."

"Wow!" I say, "we thought of at least three more reformulations for these books, and you may think of others. Right now, think about which reformulation you might try," pointing to my display of graphic representations on the whiteboard. "Tell your partner." I circulate to hear students' ideas. "When you're ready, turn to a new page in your reading response notebook and get started."

Now students get to work, and Lauren and I again circulate, conferring with students to use the texts and the appropriate graphic representation for the reformulation they chose. We again notice students doing close reading, underlining details, as they fill in their graphic representations, sharing their work with neighbors as they go. They are addressing state and national standards for informational reading, such as interpreting information visually, orally, and quantitatively, and explaining how their visual displays contribute to an understanding of the text overall. The following are examples of reformulations students create that day. In Figure 30a, Ella makes a flow map that shows the process of making jam, candy, syrup, and wine from the saguaro fruit. In Figure 30b, Marcello shows the animals that are active before, during, and after the cactus's life span. At the bottom of his display is a color-coded timeline, with each colored square representing one kind of animal, providing a quick comparison of how many kinds of animals live in the cactus before, during, and after its life span. Figures 31a and b show Maribel's line graph of the cactus's growth and then what she notices about this growth pattern. In all instances, students use creative ways to deepen their understanding of desert life and the saguaro cactus. More important, the process taught students how to make intentional choices about ways to respond to a text that match their purposes for exploring and deepening their understanding as they read. This became an emerging understanding of their use of the reader response notebook as the first months of school came to an end. In Chapter 4, I show how we build on this emerging intentionality to develop students' sense of agency, autonomy, and accountability in their use of the RRN.

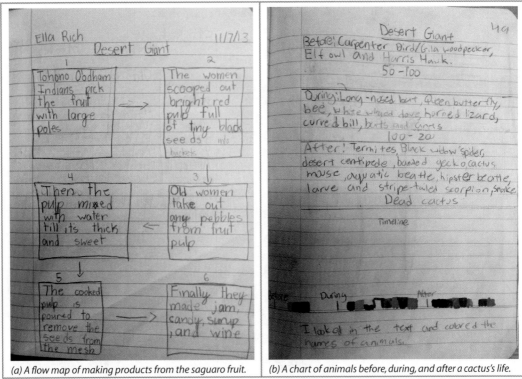

(a) A flow map of making products from the saguaro fruit.

(b) A chart of animals before, during, and after a cactus's life.

FIGURE 30. Two examples of diagrams.

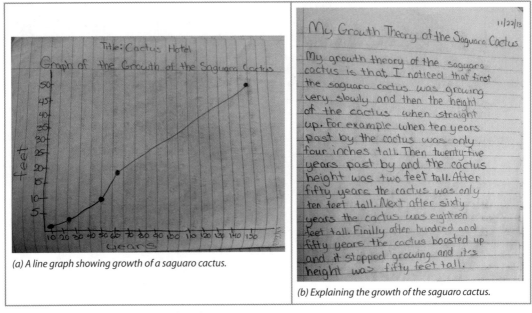

(a) A line graph showing growth of a saguaro cactus.

(b) Explaining the growth of the saguaro cactus.

FIGURE 31. Maribel's line graph and explanation.

How to Support Reluctant Responders

We all have them in our classrooms each year—students who seem disengaged or unmotivated or unwilling to do the work. In the case of reluctant responders, here's some advice.

First, find out why they are stuck. Is it the particular strategy we are practicing? Is it because the student doesn't know how to apply the strategy to the text that he or she is reading? Is it because the student is disengaged from the text?

The particular strategy is causing the reluctance.	• Good news! In our approach to RRNs, we use an unlimited number of ways to respond (see Appendix C and Chapter 5), so as the teacher, I truly don't worry too much if one way of responding doesn't appeal to a student. • I can support a student's application of a new strategy in one-on-one and small group conferences (see Chapter 4). • Students sometimes learn to like a response strategy during share sessions, when they see how other students have used it (see Chapter 4).
The student doesn't know how to apply the strategy to the text he or she is reading.	• Not to worry! It's likely that we'll use this strategy again for other texts. • I can support a student's application of a new strategy in one-on-one and small group conferences (see Chapter 4). • Students can seek support from their reading partners or in small groups (see Chapter 4).
The student is disengaged from the text.	• That happens! We don't always engage with every text we read, and it's difficult to respond meaningfully to a text we feel disengaged from. • I can confer one on one with the student to find out why he or she feels disengaged. The beginning of a book is sometimes ambiguous and confusing. Sometimes it takes a few chapters for the text to grow on us. At the least, I'll gain a better understanding of what texts are "better fits" for this student. • In a one-on-one conference, we can try the strategy on a text that the student likes (keeping in mind popular culture texts as well!).
Other considerations.	• In a balanced literacy framework, there are enough practices to support every student's engagement and motivation: interactive read-aloud, shared reading, independent reading, partnership reading, guided reading, book clubs. All of these practices support reader response. Implementing these practices consistently across each week will increase the likelihood that a reluctant responder will find an entry point for reader response. • I show in Chapter 4 how our RRN work becomes an integral part of the classroom community. If you establish a caring community, the reluctant responder will more likely want to join the literacy club, valuing what the community values. • By opening up response to choice, tools, drawing and design, by encouraging creativity, and connecting response to purpose, reluctant responders are much more likely to find an entry point for reader response.

Toward Agency, Autonomy, and Accountability

Share Sessions

From the start of every classroom collaboration with teachers and students, we conduct share sessions so that students understand that their notebook responses aren't just for the teacher, but also for social engagement with classmates around their reading lives. Now that students were learning to make intentional choices about ways to respond that matched their purposes for exploring and deepening their understanding of texts they read, it was imperative through share sessions to expand what was possible. In one share session, I brought in some exemplary RRNs from my graduate students. In table groups, students huddled over these notebooks, taking notes on kinds of entries that intrigued them. They used sticky notes to mark entries they wanted to discuss. After ten minutes, students passed the notebook they'd been reading, so after thirty minutes, they all got to peruse three different notebooks. For the next ten minutes, students shared with the whole class entry ideas they loved and might like to try. In the final minutes of the period, we instructed students to try one of these responses for any text they were currently reading. I realize that most teachers don't have access to notebooks of graduate students, but after one year of implementing the RRN as described in this book, you will have some exemplary notebooks to show new students. This is, in fact, what we did after the first year of this work, and it made a bigger impact because new students were perusing notebooks of peers.

Table 2 describes the various share sessions that teachers use with their students throughout the year. We always first give students time to reread and identify entries they want to share. Figure 32 is an example of third grader Terrence preparing an entry for a share session. These sessions convey the values of agency and autonomy, but also accountability to the community. By regularly sharing entries with classmates, students realize that their entries have to be insightful about the texts that are important in their lives.

TABLE 2. Kinds of Share Sessions

Share Session	How It Works
Partner Share	Students share entries with their reading partner.
Exemplary Notebook Share	Bring in six or more exemplary notebooks (one for each table group) from previous years. Table groups study one notebook, then swap notebooks with another table every ten minutes.
Table Share	Students share entries with their tablemates. Students leave one another sticky notes that express positive and specific feedback.
Pass the Notebook	Students look through a classmate's RRN for a designated time period (three to five minutes), then pass the notebook.
Whole-Class Share	Sitting in a whole-class circle, standing in front of the class, or using the document camera, selected students share entries from their notebooks.
"Speed Dating"	Students arrange opposing chairs in rows. They share with the person across from them for a designated time period (three minutes), then rotate clockwise to face a new partner.
Fishbowl	One group sits in the middle and replays their discussion. The rest of the class sits on the periphery of the circle, observing and taking notes of this group's strengths and needs, based on established criteria.
Quaker Share	Whole class sits in a circle around the perimeter of the classroom. Anyone can share an entry in random order. No comments, no questions, no applause. No one is called on and no one is obligated to share. Share session ends when, after ten seconds of silence, no one new wants to share.

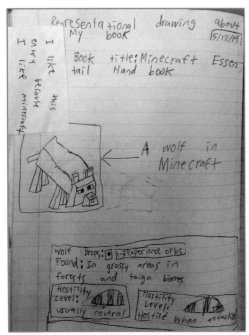

FIGURE 32. Preparing for a share session.

Our favorite share session is what the students themselves called "speed dating." We first tell students to mark three to five favorite entries with sticky notes. Favorite entries are entries in which they loved the text they responded to, they loved how they responded to a text, they surprised themselves with their thinking, they were innovative in the way they responded, or they were particularly proud of the response they made. In this format, we have students line up their chairs facing each other in one or two rows (depending on the number of students) along the length of the classroom (see Figure 33). Students get three minutes to share with the person across from them. At the halfway mark, we remind them to "make sure your partner now has a turn." At three minutes, the timer goes off, and students rotate one seat clockwise; then, on a signal, they share with their new partner. In this way, after a little more than twenty-one minutes (some time is taken for transitions), students share entries with seven other students, gaining a wide range of ideas for ways to respond in their notebooks. As in most share sessions, we then encourage students to try one of the new ideas they gained for a text they are currently reading. After each session, we also ask students to keep an ongoing

FIGURE 33. "Speed dating" in action.

list of ideas they might want to try. Over time, students end up with several pages of ideas. Figure 34 provides two pages of a list that a third grader in Lori Diamond's class kept.

New Ideas

1. Write poems
2. Write mini stories (TRUE)
3. Underline important phrases
4. Write summaries
5. Write summary boxes
6. Write an obituary
7. Write the 5 senses   15. T-charts
8. Write diagrams!!   16. Timeline
9. Write letters   17. Relating to
   your character
10. Cast of characters   18. Relationship
11. Cast of places   A. H charts
12. Venn Diagram
13. Plot Summary
14. Favorite Parts

New Ideas (continued)

20. Movie to book connections
21. Writing Quotes
22. Realistic pictures
23. Stop and Jot
24. Make and answer questions
25. Explain a story

26. Sketch to Stretch
27. Response to poems
28. Relationship web
29. Response to a movie
30. Talking about something long ago
31. Make a mood web according to each chapter

FIGURE 34. A two-page list of a third grader's RRN response ideas.

Grading Criteria

Once students become comfortable using the RRN (somewhere around mid-October to early November), we are ready to apply grading criteria. This is a controversial decision. After all, we want students to have agency and autonomy over their use of the RRN, and now we are imposing accountability by and for the teacher. Moreover, as already mentioned, we believe that through share sessions, students gain accountability to the community, which we consider the truest form of accountability because students want to impress their classmates with their insights and creativity and the reading lives that shape their identity. But teachers are also accountable to a larger community that influences classroom life, namely, parents and administrators. Grading criteria should provide unambiguous measures of each student's performance for these groups who have a vested interest in students' progress.

Most important, we believe assessment should be done *with* students, not *to* students. We value a feedback loop, whereby students understand the criteria for excellent performance, can identify where they are in terms of these criteria, and know what steps to take to raise their performance. By negotiating criteria for excellence with students and then providing clear and consistent feedback, they gain insight into what they are doing well and what and how they might improve. This feedback loop develops agency and can encourage autonomy under the right conditions. What are the right conditions? We assert that the right conditions include appropriate levels of challenge, while promoting creativity; a dialogic classroom community as depicted in our share sessions; and high levels of trust between teachers and students and among students. In *Visible Learning for Literacy, Grades K–12*, Fisher, Frey, and Hattie (2016) state: "Positive relationships are fostered and maintained when teachers set fair expectations, involve students in determining aspects of classroom organization and management, and hold students accountable for the expectations in equitable ways" (p. 13). Overall, we want our students to "gain a reputation as great learners not only in [our] eyes but also in the eyes of their peers" (p. 15).

The teachers and I have four categories of excellence in mind when we think of the reading response notebooks: **maintenance, volume, variety**, and **thoughtfulness**. We first discussed these categories as a group. What do we want to see from our students in each of these categories? The answer was: it depends. It depends on the grade level, the range of skills and learning needs of our students, and their level of experience with the use of the notebook.

With this variability in mind, the teachers and I established some common ground for criteria in each category. Under *maintenance*, for example, we know that we don't want students to use this notebook like any other school notebook; we want them to treat the notebook with care. This means perhaps decorating the cover, writing the date on top of each new entry, starting each entry on a new page, writing the title of the text, not skipping pages, not tearing pages out, not using the notebook for any other purpose, using tabs for ongoing lists, perhaps numbering each entry, showing evidence of best spelling and proofreading, and working neatly. For *volume*, we want to see an average of three responses each week. We are aware that some entries might be just a few lines, while others might be a few pages long, and yet other entries might show lots of attention to design elements. For *variety*, we want to see many kinds of entries for many kinds of texts. Some entries might consist only of words; other entries might use words in combination with page design; some entries might be predominantly design with few or no words.

Thoughtfulness required the most discussion by our group. How would we know when students were being thoughtful in their entries? We want to see more than one entry for important texts in their lives. We want to see many ways of responding to one text. We want to see *intentionality* in each of their entries. In other words, we want students to choose a response that helps them make sense and deepen their understanding of the text they are responding to. We want entries to feel like discovery. We were now ready to negotiate criteria with our students.

With each new class, we present *our* intentions to the students. In Lori Diamond's third-grade class, we asked, "Why would we want to grade your reading response notebooks?" Students shared comments such as: so we know how we're doing; so the principal and our parents know how we're doing; so we can see if we are improving; so we can see how we can do better. Students were definitely anticipating our intentions for grading their notebooks. We then introduced the four categories and opened up each one for discussion: "What does it mean to write with *volume* (or *variety* or *thoughtfulness*)?" "What does it mean to take good care of your notebook, what we'll call *maintenance*?" We recorded their responses and developed some common language, working toward our expectations for excellent work. Later, we consolidated their responses and the next day presented the grading criteria for their RRNs. Appendix B is an example of the grading criteria. A few caveats:

- The grading criteria for each category must be negotiated with students so that the classroom community has a common understanding that isn't imposed on them. As Figure 35 shows, we regularly review qualities for RRN work.

- In addition to the grade or score, teachers either write a comment or meet one on one with each student to provide feedback.
- Notice that on the grading form, we provide feedback questions that we expect students to respond to. Figure 36 is an example of fourth grader Ninka's RRN grade.

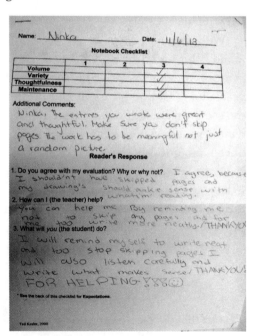

FIGURE 35. RRN rules.

- At the beginning of the school year, we establish conditions for who will read their notebooks. In some classes (such as my own), we establish that we, as their teachers, are the only other people who will read their notebooks without asking permission. In all other cases (including parents and administrators), students are in charge of what they want to share. In other classes (such as Debra Kessler's or Lesley Doff's), we establish that we will be regularly sharing our notebooks with classmates.

- As teachers we never write in our students' notebooks. Again, we want them to have ownership (autonomy). We leave sticky note comments about particular entries we read. Often students also write reflective notes (as demonstrated in Figure 37a). For Table Shares, Lesley Doff has students grade one another's notebooks (see Figure 37b).

It's clear from these examples how students are part of the process, making learning visible. Assessment is done *with* them, NOT *to* them.

FIGURE 36. Ninka's writing checklist grade.

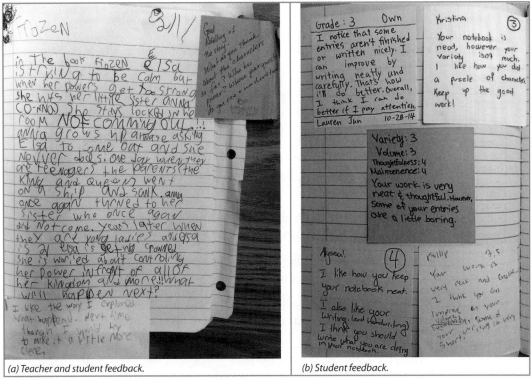

(a) Teacher and student feedback.

(b) Student feedback.

FIGURE 37. Examples of teacher and student feedback.

The teachers and I then had to figure out how to find time in our busy days to grade students' notebooks. We knew that we had to read students' notebooks regularly, perhaps every two weeks, to keep a finger on the pulse of each of their reading lives, which would then inform our teaching. Teachers decided to grade notebooks table by table. Figure 38 is an example of a grading schedule for a class with six tables of five children each, meaning teachers have only five notebooks to grade each day. Students know which day to leave their notebooks out for grad-

DAY 1	TABLE 1
DAY 2	TABLE 2
DAY 3	TABLE 3
DAY 4	TABLE 4
DAY 5	TABLE 5
DAY 6	TABLE 6

FIGURE 38. Grading schedule.

ing. The truth is, if notebooks are graded every two weeks at most, then there are only five or six new entries each time to respond to, and grading each notebook takes just a few minutes.

In the best of formative assessment, we gain so much instructional insight from reading and grading students' notebooks. I keep notes of patterns and insights I perceive for individual students and across the class. I read students' notebooks with some of the following guiding questions:

- Who has a compelling entry that others can learn from for whole-class sharing?

- Who tried an innovative entry that I might teach the whole class in a mini-lesson?

- What design choices are students making (e.g., choices of color, shapes, lines, proportion, layout, font, visual displays, graphic organizers)?

- Who has tried an entry that I want to confer with the student about?

- What am I noticing for each student and across students in terms of *volume, variety, thoughtfulness,* and *maintenance*? How might I best address these issues?

- Which students are writing NOT retrospective accounts, but instead introspective journeys (Hancock, 1993)?

- For introspective journeys, which students are thinking in a variety of ways about one important text?

- Which students are writing about many kinds of text (not just school books, but also popular culture texts and texts in many kinds of media)?

- What kinds of ongoing lists are students keeping? Who might benefit from knowing about some of the ongoing lists that classmates are keeping?

- How might I use students' responses to shape and inform curriculum?

Later in this chapter, I share some of the ways our insights about RRN entries inform instruction for mini-lessons, conferences, and small- and whole-class discussions.

A Reading Response Checklist

It was after reading students' notebooks in mid-November that we realized students were clinging to a few "tried and true" response strategies and not taking risks with less familiar or innovative responses. In other words, they were scoring low on the *variety* of ways they might respond to texts. "What can we do about it?" we asked. Within a few minutes of discussion, we came up with a student checklist to encourage more variety. Appendix A is the checklist we developed. See Figure 39 for two examples of checklists in use by fourth-grade students in Lauren Heinz and Debra Kessler's classes.

NAME:	Date	Date	Date	Date
Sketch-to-Stretch	5/5/14	5/2/14		
Summary Boxes	4/2/14	4/29/14	4/30/14	6/3/14
Representational Drawing	4/2/14			
Character List	4/29/14			
Character Web of Relationships	5/2/14	5/23/14		
The Subtext Strategy	5/7/14			
Writing the Blurb	5/1/14	5/29/14		
A letter to the character, to the author, or between characters	5/1/14	6/11/14	6/13/14	
Reformulations- Chart, Graph, Diagram	5/2/14	5/28/14	6/10/14	
Critical Literacy- Writing from the perspective of a character that has a limited voice	4/30/14	5/2/14		
Critical Literacy- Asking questions of characters	5/3/14			
Critical Literacy- Writing a letter from one character to another.	5/2/14			
Critical Literacy- Writing "the untold story": what is NOT said in the text that should be said				
Found Poetry	4/30/14			
Leaning In	5/8/14			
Digging In	5/5/14			
Lifting a Line	5/18/14			
Other: Powerline	4/30/14	5/25/14		
Other: main idea and details	6/4/14			
Other:				
Ongoing lists:				

(Just started writing on here on April 2014)

Readers Notebook Strategies

NAME: Nina	Date	Date	Date	Date
Sketch-to-Stretch	4/10/14	5/5/14	5/7/14	
Summary Boxes				
Representational Drawing	4/28/14	5/7/14	5/5/14	
Character List	5/5/14	5/9/14	5/9/14	5/12/14
Character Web of Relationships	4/11/14	5/8/14	5/12/14	5/12/14
The Subtext Strategy				
Writing the Blurb	5/22/14	5/21/14	5/28/14	5/28/14 6/2/14
A letter to the character, to the author, or between characters	5/7/14			
Reformulations- Chart, Graph, Diagram	4/10/14 4/10/14	5/20/14	5/28/14	5/29/14
Critical Literacy- Writing from the perspective of a character that has a limited voice	5/5/14 wretched stone	5/8/14		5/29/14 6/2/14 6/4/14 4/11/14
Critical Literacy- Asking questions of characters				
Critical Literacy- Writing a letter from one character to another.	5/28/14			
Critical Literacy- Writing "the untold story": what is NOT said in the text that should be said				
Found Poetry				
Leaning In				
Digging In				
Lifting a Line				
Other: Letter to Restaurant	5/28/14			
Other:				
Other:				
Ongoing lists:				

FIGURE 39. Examples of RRN strategy checklists.

Notice the spaces on these checklists for students to include "other" strategies that they invented or learned from sharing with classmates. The checklist emphasizes the variety of responses we value in our communities of practice. We found that this tool reminded students to be expansive in their use of reader response strategies, promoting agency, autonomy, and accountability.

Conferences

One way we develop the quality of students' RRN work is through one-on-one and small-group conferences. For conferences, we follow the structure articulated by Carl Anderson (2000) in *How's It Going?* Figure 40 provides an overview of the conference structure. Our conferences begin with **researching** the reader for strengths and needs. For our purposes, students' RRN work provides powerful sources of research. By reading their notebooks on a consistent schedule, we are able to come to conferences with strong ideas already in mind. From this research emerges a **compliment** and **teaching point**. As Anderson explains, the compliment is not cursory. By noticing and naming what students are doing well, we reinforce those behaviors for perpetuity, strengthening student agency and autonomy. The teaching point names for the student the gaps in his or her work toward our negotiated criteria, why this matters, and how to achieve stronger performance. We **teach** the student to achieve this performance with **guided practice**. This is performance in the student's zone of proximal development (ZPD), performing with the assistance of a more competent partner what the student is not yet able to do on his or her own (Vygotsky, 1978). In a socially mediated, goal-oriented activity, students appropriate the regulatory means of accomplishing the activity, infusing it with their own intentions. Finally, once we observe approximation toward higher performance, we **link** this work to the student's ongoing, independent work.

STRUCTURE OF A CONFERENCE

Research:
- Observe.
- Interview with content questions, process questions, clarifying questions.
- Read student response notebooks.

Decide: What to teach; how to teach it

Compliment:
- Compliment something the reader/writer is *just* starting to do by naming what the reader/writer is doing and *how* she or he is or may be doing it.

Teach (like a mini-lesson):
- Give the purpose for the strategy you're about to teach.
- Name the strategy you will teach (teaching point).
- Teach the strategy through demonstration, explanation and example, inquiry, guided practice.

Guided Practice:
- Get the student to try the strategy in front of you.

Link:
- Restate the compliment and the teaching point.
- Link to student's ongoing work.

FIGURE 40. Structure of a conference.

Here is an example of a conference using the RRN as a socially mediated, goal-oriented tool for thinking. Lori Diamond's third-grade class of twenty-eight students was learning how to infer character traits and interactions. It was independent reading time. Stefan wrote the entry in Figure 41 about Willy Wonka. Stefan was an ELL student from Pakistan whose primary language was Punjabi. He wrote: "Mr. Wonka is funny. He tried to trick the president. He is a persuasive guy. He stopped people to put him in trouble." The picture shows Mr. Wonka, labeled "Wonka," and in a speech bubble, Mr. Wonka exclaims, "ZonkZonkZonkZonkZonk!" Next to a gate is a sign: "Visit us!" Lori felt that this response was sparse, with too little elaboration to show Willy Wonka's key character traits, and she wanted to see if Stefan could express a more central characteristic of Mr. Wonka. She also felt that Stefan might express this understanding best if he could "put himself in Mr. Wonka's shoes" by writing in the voice of Mr. Wonka, a response strategy we had tried with other texts. She convened the conference with Stefan. In the following transcript, I add commentary in the margins to highlight some of Lori's key instructional moves. I also provide time intervals so you can see how the conference structure enables a focused and efficient exchange.

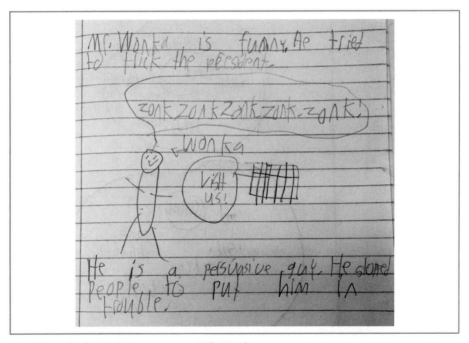

FIGURE 41. Stefan's initial response to Willy Wonka.

LORI DIAMOND: Stefan, I like how you wrote two characteristics about Mr. Wonka: he's funny and he's persuasive, and you knew to give examples of for each one. [Points to these parts in his writing.] What did you show in your picture? [Points to the picture.]

> LD notices and names what Stefan has done successfully (a **compliment**) and inquires further by asking Stefan about his drawing.

STEFAN: Well, he says funny things, like "ZonkZonkZonkZonkZonk!" And he is welcoming, like this sign, "Visit us!"

LD: Okay, so I want to show you a different strategy for you to show your thinking and learning about Mr. Wonka and your thinking about him as a character. If you were going to describe Mr. Wonka to somebody else, um, let's say you were—what's the name of the little boy?

> LD introduces the teaching point, but first continues with more **research**: can Stefan perceive a central characteristic of Mr. Wonka?

STEFAN: Charlie.

LD: Charlie. So, let's say you were Charlie, and you were going to tell your friends at school what Mr. Wonka was about, what would you say? [Pause.] What kind of person is he? [Pause.]

STEFAN: Well, if I ever went to school after that [experience at the chocolate factory; LD nods her head in approval], I would tell my friends that he's, he is amazingly open, with new ideas and proposals.

> LD recognizes that Stefan just made an inference about Charlie's future. She hears that Stefan recognizes a key characteristic of Mr. Wonka: he is inventive and creative, amazingly open, with new ideas and proposals. This realization is part of her **research** into which strategy she now might teach Stefan to use.

LD: Wow! He's really done that. He's really tried to show Charlie about being more open. Right?

> LD acknowledges Stefan's thinking while she **decides** what to teach.

STEFAN: Yeah.

LD: I like how you identified a character trait of Mr. Wonka that is important to the entire story. You not only named a character trait but also have ideas about why this matters to the story. [Stefan nods in recognition.] Stefan, we're going to try some new strate-

> LD gives another **compliment** that lifts the level of what Stefan should continue to do as he thinks about central characters.

gies that you can use to maybe do this a little differently, to talk about Mr. Wonka as a character and really show your thinking, your best thinking, and I want you to think about whether or not, if you can stand in somebody else's shoes, if you can kinda <u>become</u> the character. So, if you were going to <u>become</u> Mr. Wonka, who would you have a conversation with? Who would you try to <u>convince</u> that your thinking was the best thinking?

LD now **teaches** a strategy of "putting yourself in the character's shoes." She believes this will deepen Stefan's thinking about the central character, Mr. Wonka. She guides Stefan toward his response with a series of guiding questions.

STEFAN: I'd try to convince Grandma Georgina because she was trying to <u>stop</u> me [he thrusts out his open left hand, a gesture for <u>stop</u>]. She was not open to new adventures, new ideas.

LD: Okay, so, I'm going to ask you to write a letter to, or have a <u>conversation</u> with, Grandma Georgina about how she should be more open to ideas. Okay, Stefan, can

LD observes Stefan's successful attempt at this strategy.

you try to do that? [Stefan nods yes. LD watches for thirty seconds as Stefan gets started.] Great. I'll check in later to see how it went. [LD moves on to another conference.]

Total Time: 3 min. 13 sec.

Later during independent reading, Lori checked in with Stefan. Figure 42 is his revised response, which certainly shows more elaborate thinking. He expresses a more central characteristic of Mr. Wonka by writing in his voice, directly addressing Grandma Georgina. Moreover, he shows an understanding of key behaviors—lethargy and skepticism—that are too often characteristic of elderly people like Grandma Georgina. Lori then had the following brief exchange with Stefan:

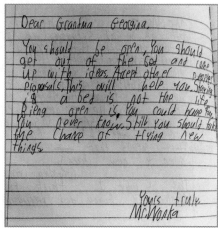

FIGURE 42. Stefan's revised response to Willy Wonka.

LD: Wow! I like how you were able to "put yourself in Mr. Wonka's shoes" to show one of his characteristics that is so important to the story. That was a good choice to write to Grandma Georgina because Mr. Wonka ends up giving her important advice. So, did this strategy help?

LD again provides a specific compliment by noticing and naming what Stefan is now doing successfully. She prompts for Stefan's metacognition.

Stefan: Yes, because I had to really think like Mr. Wonka and imagine what he would say to Grandma Georgina.

LD: Yes, Stefan, I agree. So this is definitely a response strategy you could use when you want to think deeply about characters in stories. Okay? [Stefan nods in approval.]

> LD now **links** the strategy to Stefan's ongoing work of inferring about characters.

Total Time: 37 sec.

Total Conference Time: 3 min. 50 sec.

What's also interesting about this conference is that it was divided into two parts. Once she saw that Stefan understood how to apply this new strategy, Lori knew she didn't need to sit by his side as he wrote his response. Instead, she was able to circulate, confer with other students, and then return to Stefan for a brief follow-up to link the strategy to his ongoing work. In addition, as mentioned earlier, this was a strategy we had taught the students, which may be why Stefan was able to apply it so readily once Lori reminded him of it. He clearly needed that prompting within his zone of proximal development to now apply it to his independent reading (Stage 3 of Figure 11). In general, one-on-one conferences provide a powerful structure to work within each student's ZPD, using the RRN as a mediational tool to lift the student's level of performance.

Partnerships and Small-Group Work

It was early November when Jen Sussman and I first taught her twenty-eight second graders the strategy of reformulation (see Chapter 3). Let's take another look at the activities surrounding one of the books, *Cactus Hotel* (Guiberson & Lloyd, 1991), that Jen introduced in a read-aloud and then followed up by providing each student with a typed copy of the text. On this day, we provide two reformulation choices, a diagram or a timeline, which we present in a mini-lesson, to show the life of the giant saguaro cactus. In our mini-lesson, we show examples of diagrams and timelines in nonfiction books from the classroom library to emphasize features such as labels and headings. However, here's what's interesting: we deliberately avoid discussing *how* to create a diagram or timeline, because we also want to see what children will do on their own, as a sort of formative assessment, and to inform our instruction going forward about what we might need to teach students about these visual displays. Instead, with their copies of the text, we guide them in circling and starring places that describe the cactus and underlining passages of time with the size of the cactus. Students get into their pairings and groups of three and spread out around the room, working at tables, in corners, or on the hardwood floor. They have their RRNs, drawing and writing tools, and rulers. Jen and I believe that when the reader response notebook is used as a mediational tool, students lift one another's level of performance when working collaboratively toward a goal-directed activity (Vygotsky, 1978). Purposeful activity includes writing, talking, and understanding others and their perspectives, as well as using reading to get things done and to think and act in new ways.

Sue and Charlie are working on the floor. They have decided to make a timeline of the cactus's growth across its lifetime. They are scanning the text for evidence.

"Let's read it quickly, faster, so we can move on [with their timeline]," Charlie says. He points to one of the paragraphs that describes passage of time and the size of the cactus. "It's right here." He points to the paragraph that says, *After sixty years, the cactus hotel is eighteen feet tall.* Sue now scans that paragraph with her right index finger. Both of them hunch over the text, pointing with their right index fingers and reading aloud.

"Fifty feet tall [after 150 years]!" Charlie exclaims. Sue starts to draw the cactus for the final part of her timeline but runs into trouble. She drew her timeline starting only one-third of the way down the page, so there's not enough room. When the cactus is 18 feet after sixty years, her drawing of the cactus already reaches the top of the page.

FIGURE 43. Sue draws her timeline.

Fifty! Ahh! Sue pauses, and then fills in her drawing of the cactus at sixty years (see Figure 43). "How would a 50 feet be tall?"

Charlie stops working on his drawing and looks at Sue. "Okay, that's the tallest one."

Sue reaches over Charlie and grabs the 12-inch ruler. She holds it vertically against the floor with her right hand, marks the end point with her left hand, places the ruler at her right hand, and moves her left hand up to the top of the ruler: "One, two" (see Figure 44).

As Sue continues to measure up, Charlie exclaims, "That's like two classrooms!" (Indeed, in their older school building, the ceiling of their classroom was perhaps 18 feet tall.)

FIGURE 44. Sue measures 50 feet tall.

Now Sue stands up. "You're never gonna do that. It's like 18 feet up to the top." Sue gets to 5 feet. She is standing on tippy toes reaching up with the ruler and her arms. She smiles. "Ahh! I can't touch it!" (the ceiling). She turns to Charlie, "You do it!" Charlie shakes his head, implying it's ridiculous, and instead draws an incomplete cactus to the top of his page with an arrow going up. Next to the arrow he writes, "50 feet." Sue looks at Charlie's solution and does the same for her drawing.

Wow! There's so much to say about the collaborative nature of this partnership work that led to such deeper understanding of the life cycle of the saguaro cactus. First, Jen trusted the students in their process of problem solving. Sue and Charlie had the opportunity to play while they worked. Sue's face in Figure 44 shows joyful learning as she used the ruler to imagine 50 feet tall, and Charlie tolerated her exploration, even though he wanted to move on. Second, Vygotsky (1978) was always clear that the zone of proximal development is a space of disequilibrium and incongruity, where what a child is now processing doesn't fit with what the child already knows and can perform independently. It's in the desire to resolve this discrepancy that learning occurs. By trusting her students, Jen gave them the time and space they needed to confront and resolve these incongruities. Third, this partnership illustrates the power and possibility of collaborative learning when students are working through a joint goal-directed activity. Charlie pointed out the relevant passage in the text, he and Sue did close reading of the information together, they played together to imagine the cactus giant, and they came up with one solution for how to represent its size after 150 years. They achieved their timeline. This process led to much deeper learning than would have occurred if Jen had emphasized "the correct way to make a timeline."

Small-Group Discussions

In the previous section, I showed that when students work in partnerships or small groups through a meaningful, goal-directed activity, their notebook responses become mediational tools for generative thinking about texts. In other words, rather than only the teacher or a more competent peer providing support within the zone of proximal development, sources of support that lead students toward higher levels of performance become more distributed among the learning community (see Kesler, Gibson, Turansky, 2016). This is also what occurred as students worked in reading clubs or small share groups to discuss their reader responses. Sometimes students prepare for small-group discussions by generating talk questions, as in Figure 45. We then coach small groups in developing ways to extend their ensuing discussion as they address one or more of their questions.

More often, small groups share and discuss their reader responses to texts. In Lori Diamond's third-grade class, for example, they were reading aloud *Because of Winn-Dixie* (DiCamillo, 2000). The class had worked on a character list, coding key characters (as specified in Chapter 3). Today, we wanted students to use their drawing tools to explore a character web of relationships (also as specified in Chapter 3). After twenty minutes of work, we instructed students to form their small groups to share their work. I listened in to a group of five girls: Denise, Meilin, Jasmine, Cheryl, and Jhoyti. Denise was sharing her character web (Figure 46). In the following dialogue, I again add commentary in the margins of the transcript to highlight some of the ways this group of girls and I used distributive cognition to mediate deeper understandings of character relationships.

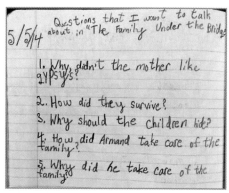

FIGURE 45. Discussion questions for *The Family under the Bridge.*

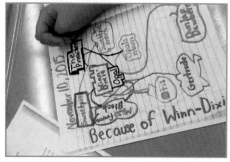

FIGURE 46. Denise's character web of relationships for *Because of Winn-Dixie.*

DENISE: The preacher loves his, Opal's mom [her right index finger points out this pathway on her web], and Opal's mom [now her right index finger vibrates over "Opal's mom" and then traces the pathway to Opal] loves, loves, uh, Opal, and Opal is together with Winn-Dixie, so I joined them together. [Pause. She seems done with sharing.]

ME: Anything more you're gonna do with that? Are you <u>done</u>, or is there more you were going to do with that if you had more time?

DENISE: Yeah. More.

ME: Like what?

DENISE: Like I'll make a key [her right index finger circles key names on her web] to explain why [her right index finger

> I noticed that Denise's entry lacked a legend. In addition, Denise seemed done sharing. Instead, I wanted to emphasize revision of thinking during dialogic interactions.

now flows from name to name]. . . . I want to do a <u>key</u> for like, why Winn-Dixie has red color and the preacher has black and why Stevie Dewberry is yellow and why Miss Fanny Belch is different kind of colors.

ME: [to the group] Did you guys notice how I asked a question? [They nod.] Okay. So you can ask questions of the person, or say, "I like how you did this" or "that was a good idea to do this" or, you can <u>comment</u> on each other's work. Okay? Who wants to go next?

[There's an awkward pause as Jhoyti seems to want to share. They all look at her. Now Denise points to the key on Jhoyti's web as she reads Jhoyti's codes. Jhoyti's code for The Preacher states, "Turtle" (see Figure 47).]

DENISE: Why'd you do the preacher in turtle color? [Points between the code and The Preacher.]

CHERYL: Turquoise.

JHOYTI: Um, 'cause Opal sometimes describes the Preacher as a turtle [pause] -ish. [Now writes -ish in the bottom of her legend in pencil next to *turtle*.] And I wrote Opal is . . .

[Denise reaches over and points at Gertrude on the web.]

DENISE: Gertrude.

JHOYTI: She's the parrot.

[Denise points back to the legend.]

DENISE: Oh, so the parrot's blind.

The girls were used to monologic talk, even in small groups: each person takes a turn, usually in order, without ever building on one another's ideas. My prompts were intended to jump-start more dialogic interactions.

I restrained myself, and the girls came through. Denise initiates more dialogic interaction, using Jhoyti's web as a mediational tool.

FIGURE 47. Jhoyti's character web of relationships for *Because of Winn-Dixie*.

Did Jhoyti mean *turquoise* or *turtle color* or perhaps both? Does it matter? What this exchange shows is the provisional and generative nature of dialogic interaction as the girls use their responses as mediational tools for thinking.

JHOYTI: No. What? [Looks at where Denise is pointing.] This is a box [pointing to her legend]; it's just a booooxxxxx [circling the legend, as a way to explain the discrepancy with her choice of brown color for Gertrude.]

> Jhoyti is held accountable to the group, which expects warrantable interpretations. In this context, Jhoyti is now recognizing the need for revision of her thinking, such as adding -ish or other details to her box.

[Now Jasmine points between Gloria Dump and down to Dunlap Dewberry on Jhoyti's web.]

JASMINE: Why is Gloria Dump connected to Dunlap?

JHOYTI: Whaaaaa? [Hesitates with a response.] Well, she knows the Dewberry boys tease Opal, and she wants Opal to make friends with them, so she's making a connection.

> In the video of this group work, you can almost feel Jhoyti's brain churning as she generates new understandings about these relationships, using her own response as a mediational tool.

Now the sharing began to open up and become more fluid. Here is another segment of their sharing, a few minutes later.

CHERYL: [Circling her placement of Otis on her web; see Figure 48.] Well, I kinda put Otis on the outside because he's not really that connected [gestures with her right hand to show the cluster of other characters] to that many people, so he would sorta be, he wouldn't be, like, on the inside, because he's not, in the book, it seems like he never leaves the pet shop.

> Cheryl's web on the right side of the page (11/10/15) is a revision of her response on the left side of the page (11/9/15). On her new version, Otis is shown in yellow.

JASMINE: I put him at the bottom, sorta away from all the other characters. I did teardrops for him [to create the box surrounding his name] to show that he's always saaaaad, and that he's <u>peaceful</u>. [Meilin now corrects the spelling from *Odis* to *Otis* with a pencil, after seeing how her group members spelled his name.] He's sorta mopey.

> Jasmine builds on Cheryl's idea of Otis as an outsider, and adds to it by showing her symbolic representation of his sadness.
>
> Group participation held Meilin accountable for the correct spelling of Otis in her entry.

MEILIN: I did blue for Otis because he went to jail, so I think he's kinda sad, **and because**

JASMINE: **We sorta** did like the same thing.

Meilin: Yeah. He keeps to himself, and he doesn't really like to talk about it.

> Now Meilin uses color as another dimension to infer about Otis (blue as sad). Bold in this transcript shows overlapping speech. Jasmine literally overlaps with Meilin in their thinking about Otis's state of mind.

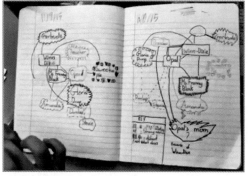

FIGURE 48. Cheryl's character web of relationships for *Because of Winn-Dixie*.

It's worth highlighting how much meaning the girls generated from the symbols and design features in their visual displays: circling Otis's name with teardrops, placing his name at the bottom of the page or apart from the cluster of other names, using a particular color to convey meaning. In other segments of their discussion, Jasmine pointed out her choice of symbols and colors for Dunlap and Stevie Dewberry, "because they're always kinda <u>harsh</u> on Opal." Cheryl then pointed out how "I sorta made them matching because they're like always together against Opal." On and on their exchanges went like this, deepening their character analysis through the provisional and generative use of symbols and design, or what Anne Haas Dyson (2003a) calls "symbol weaving."

All told, the girls' character webs of relationships for *Because of Winn-Dixie* provided a mediational tool for provisional and generative thinking during dialogic interaction. They showed distributive cognition in the zone of proximal development—in other words, each of their thinking about character relationships in *Because of Winn-Dixie* deepened and expanded as a result of their discussion. Their exchanges sometimes felt and sounded as though they were inventing understanding on the spot, such as Jhoyti's explanation of her "turtle color." We saw in action the dialogic role of reader response: "The process of reading is a mediating act with a dialogic function: The students' thoughts both shape and [a]re shaped by the articulated texts they compose" (Smagorinksy, 2001, p. 152).

Whole-Class Discussions

The kind of distributive cognition that we saw among the group of five girls in Lori Diamond's third grade can also happen in whole-class discussions, when more students can participate in active listening and speaking. First, let's look at how the teachers set up conditions for whole-class discussion. In Jen Sussman's second-grade classroom, reader response time is over and it's time to gather twenty-eight students, who are in small-group clusters all over the classroom, to the meeting area for whole-class discussion. Jen rings the chime signaling students to stop, look, and listen. When the class shows their full attention, she poses the following question: "How can we gather in the meeting area in such a way that everyone can see and hear each other and participate?" This is a review of behaviors they have practiced many times. Students raise their hands to respond. She calls on Hae Ran: "We can sit in a circle facing each other." Jen nods in acknowledgment. "We will be sharing our response work, so what will you need?" Charlie responds: "Our notebooks?" William adds, ". . . and something to write with in case we want to make any changes." Jen then asks, "How long should it take for you to be prepared for our discussion?" Daniel says, "Three minutes?" Jen estimates the necessary amount of cleanup of rulers and drawing and writing materials and negotiates the time down to a minute and a half. Then she sets the timer and observes her students make this transition.

Two moves are notable in Jen's exchange. First, Jen avoids imposing what she wants and expects, instead choosing a stance of negotiation, making her students part of the process in order to build their agency, autonomy, and accountability to the community of learners. Second, she takes an inquiry stance to observe and take note of what students are doing well and what they can improve as they make this transition. Then, when they gather in the meeting area, she has students analyze their performance: "How'd you do with this transition? What did you do well? What can you do better?" As an observer, I can report that the students held one another accountable for getting to the meeting area before "time was up," and the entire class made it on time. Jen quietly signals for certain children to sit near her so she can monitor and support their participation. Figure 49 shows the class gathered in the meeting area for their discussion.

Now that they're gathered, Jen prepares students for discussion. "We're going to share our work. We <u>cannot</u> do that if people in the circle are doing other things while people are talking. So please close your notebooks, and you'll only have something open <u>if</u> you're one of the people who are sharing, 'cause otherwise I think that it's just a little too hard, right?, to not look and draw in your notebook.

FIGURE 49. Jen's class gathers for whole-class discussion.

So, what is a way you think that we can share and get our ideas in a way that everybody can hear and see and do?" She calls on Alyssa, who is now about to share her reader response work. Jen interjects, "Answer my question, please."

ALYSSA: Well, it might be a bit too hard if everybody's raising their hands, and you call on someone, and they go "Uch!" if they don't get it [a turn] or something. I think it should just be like, somebody stops talking and you can add on, like a real conversation.

JEN: Thumbs up if you think that's something you can try. [Scans the circle, then back to Alyssa] "Would you like to start us off?"

During the ensuing ten minutes, the students discuss their responses. Jen occasionally uses gestures to signal students to show their work or to wait for someone to finish, but mostly she takes an inquiry stance—how are the students doing with following Alyssa's suggestion of *not* raising hands to bid for a turn and instead having "a real conversation"? This is the second week of November, so again, these are behaviors the class has practiced before. Jen continues to build students' agency, autonomy, and accountability by suppressing her authority and emphasizing students' negotiation of productive behaviors.

They are discussing which reformulation strategy helped them the most in understanding *Cactus Hotel* (Guiberson & Lloyd, 1991): a timeline or a diagram. As teachers, our aim was to start emphasizing students' choice based on their purposes as readers, first by limiting their response choices to two and then by gradually expanding the choices they could make. The following exchange ensued:

FIGURE 50. Alyssa shares her work.

ALYSSA: It was confusing using a diagram 'cause I don't get how it's helping myself [gesturing with her hands towards her chest]. It could help other people. I'm not saying it can't help anyone. It just doesn't, I don't get how it works for me, me, and the timeline just works, so like, for showing growing up, I just don't get how you can make a diagram for that because a timeline gives the numbers and shows it [the growth of the cactus] so it makes more sense. [See Figure 50.]

STUDENT: A diagram only shows one period of time.

STEVEN: We did a diagram because we, we didn't want to draw too many cactuses, and we thought it was like the easiest way to do it [show the life of the cactus], like one period of time.

CATHY: But a timeline was easier to show how big the cactus grew and how many feet it grew.

HAE RAN: [Cathy's partner] . . . and which years and how long it lives . . .

CATHY: Because it gets big.

STEVEN: We didn't do a timeline 'cause, like, it goes on and on, and you can draw [circling his diagram with his right index finger], and you don't get to show different parts of like the cactus, like more, like diff—, like the nests and the holes and roots and the dirt and trees. [See Figure 51.]

FIGURE 51. Steven shares his work.

NIKEEL: So, if you draw a diagram, you can show all the details for one period of time, but if you draw a timeline [he drew a timeline], you can show the entire life cycle. . . .

OLABIR: . . . and you have to choose the one that you find the best.

[A chorus of "Yeah."]

As in other exchanges in this discussion, you can hear how the whole class was constructing an understanding of the affordances and constraints of each kind of response, and the intentions you need as a reader to choose a response that best meets your purposes. This was an imperative understanding we wanted these second graders to have in order to develop agency, autonomy, and accountability for their ongoing RRN work.

Lesley Doff's classroom was located in a small schoolyard trailer that was cramped quarters for thirty fifth graders (see Figure 52). There was certainly no room for a meeting area, so whole-class discussion happened from their desks. We read aloud *Baseball Saved Us* (Mochizuki & Lee, 1993) and provided a typed copy of the text

FIGURE 52. Lesley Doff's fifth-grade class.

Handwritten notebook response:

11/7/13

Baseball Saved Us

Baseball Supplies	What they used
Uniforms	Covers of mattresses
Bleachers	wood
Bats, balls, Gloves	Delivered by friends outside camp (in sets)
Dirt	from sand and water
Bases	? Marks in the dirt ? from mattress material
Foul lines	? Marked lines in the dirt?

I think that the people in the internment camp are really creative and smart. I think that they are creative because they made mattress covers into uniforms. Bleachers out of old wood they found. They also made bases and foul lines out of marks in the dirt

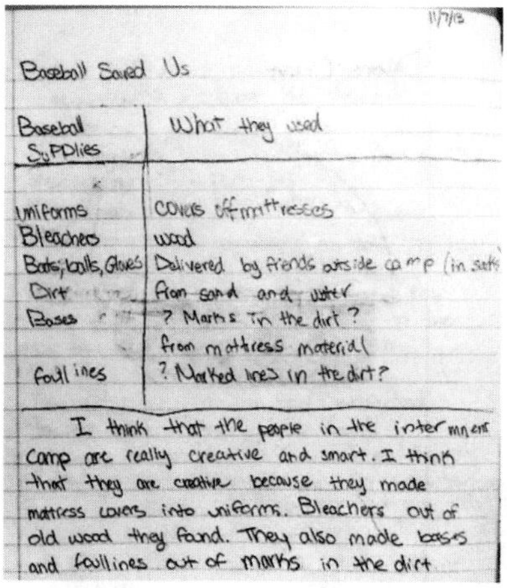

FIGURE 53. Response to *Baseball Saved Us.*

to each student. We asked the students to consider the following question: What did the incarcerated Japanese Americans need and what might they have used to play baseball with in the internment camp in the middle of the desert? "How might you show this thinking in your notebook?" we asked the students. They first worked in pairs and then shared at their tables. Most students drew a T-chart in their RRNs to sort this out (see Figure 53), using the text for evidence and relying on background knowledge about baseball and internment camps. After twenty minutes, we convened the class to discuss their ideas.

Lesley reinforces positive discussion behaviors she observed while students were working at tables, such as including everyone, speaking clearly, looking at the speaker, and referring directly to the text. "And I like that you are using and holding up your note-books to show your thinking, and that you're sharing it with the rest of your table." For the whole-class discussion, she reminds the students to be respect-ful of whoever is speaking "by giving that person our attention." She reminds them of the rules: "We don't talk over each other, we build on what each other is saying, and if you disagree, you can go in a different direction, but have some manners." She then opens up the floor for whole-class discussion.

The following discussion, with students' notebook responses as mediation-al tools, clearly deepened students' analysis of how the incarcerated Japanese Americans got the equipment they needed to play baseball. Lauren had shared the response she and Matthew made, which depicted soft canvas bases. In this exchange, Ling, referring to her own notebook response, challenges Lauren's idea about the material for the bases. For easy reference, I use numbers to mark each turn of talk.

(1) LING: Well, like the bases made out of canvas; we thought maybe they used stones? Like, put into the dirt. [Gestures downwards with both hands.]

(2) LAUREN: Um, I kinda disagree with that because, uh, people slide into bases, in baseball, and you could really hurt yourself if [**Many voices at once.**]

(3) SARAH: They don't land on the bases.

(4) JOSEPH: Lauren, but don't they have shoes?

(5) LAUREN: Uh, hands and shoes can be <u>ripped through</u>. My brother's <u>always</u> scraping himself.

(6) LING: Well, I was thinking it was different <u>flat</u> stones. [Gestures with both hands the shape of these stones.]

(7) LAUREN: Maybe, but someone could still— maybe rocks with canvas covering over it [left hand circles around to show this canvas over the flat rocks] to make it like safer. [**Many voices at once.**]

(8) LAWRENCE: I thought that they could've used, like, part of the <u>mat-tress</u>, because like baseball, uh, plates are usually like soft [gestures "soft" with his hands] and <u>cushiony</u>, so that they could slide [gestures sliding into a base with his hands] on it. [**Several voices at once.**]

(9) MIRIAM: But also the <u>bases</u> could've been that scrapped wood that fell from the houses, or they could've taken apart a mattress and taken the cotton from it, and also, somehow, taken a rock to keep it down [ges-tures a rock flattening the cotton]. [**Several voices at once.**]

(10) ANNA: Well, Lauren, how would they actually get the canvas?

(11) Lauren: Well, clothing, one. The mattress, and maybe <u>blankets</u>, which is made from really <u>soft</u> material, or maybe rough things because maybe they couldn't stuff it [a base] with materials that was really comfortable, or it could be a combination of both of them.

(12) ALEXANDER: [to Lauren] Um, I couldn't hear what you said about how the uniforms were made again?

(13) LAUREN: The uniforms were made out of, like, the bedding and the mattress [makes an offering gesture with her right hand] and sheets. [**Several voices: "Yeah." "I agree."**]

(14) DYLAN: I thought, like, the bases?, I thought it was stone, but they covered something with it [gestures covering with his hands] to make it <u>soft</u>, so they wouldn't then get seriously hurt.

(15) JOSEPH: I agree with Dylan. They coulda put a stone at the center and cotton around it and then wrap it up with canvas [right hand circles to gesture the canvas wrap].

(16) CHRIS: Yeah, the bases had to be above the ground so they could be seen, but they wouldn't be too hard to slide over [gestures sliding over with his hands].

(17) LAUREN: Well, I think they needed a little bit of weight, like Dylan said, with the rock in the middle to hold all the cushy stuff [gestures this with her right hand], because if it didn't, it could all fly away.

(18) MIRIAM: Well, also if you're running, if it's too soft when you're running to the base, you might slip on it ["Yeah"] or it might— [shows the base swept away with a foot with her hands].

(19) LAUREN: That's why you **have a rock to make it harder.**

(20) MIRIAM: **That's why you'd have the rock**, so if you push it, it stays in place.

(21) LAUREN: Yeah.

The total time of this exchange was two minutes thirty-seven seconds. There were twenty-one turns of talk by ten different students. Because the exchange built off of Lauren's notebook response, Lauren naturally had the most turns of talk (8). Notice the speculative tone the students took, with words such as *might, maybe, could, would, somehow, but,* and *if,* and the questioning tone in many of their statements. They were willing to revise their thinking, and Lauren eventually agreed that the bases might have had stone in them. Lauren and Miriam's overlapping talk (at 19 and 20 respectively) literally shows their co-constructed understanding. Lauren was able to change her mind because her classmates challenged her, returning to comments she made and asking her questions, such as Sarah and Joseph at turns 3 and 4, Anna at turn 10, and Alexander at turn 12. Likewise, Lauren challenged Ling at turn 2, and Chris (16) builds on Dylan and Joseph's thinking (14 and 15 respectively) but also challenges Ling's comment (6) that the stone bases might be flat. As a community of learners, the students held one another accountable for warrantable interpretations of the text. They clearly applied Lesley's ground rules for whole-class discussion. More important, using their notebook responses as mediational tools for thinking, they applied distributive cognition to develop stronger interpretations about *Baseball Saved Us.*

Summary

In this chapter, I show pervasive classroom practices that build agency, autonomy, and accountability. Table 3 summarizes these practices.

TABLE 3. Summary of Classroom Practices

CLASSROOM PRACTICES	COMMENTS
Explicit instruction of RRN strategies	See Chapters 2 and 3 and Figure 11 for ideas.
An anchor chart of response strategies	See Table 1 and Appendix C for details.
Assessment of notebooks	See Appendix B for details. Negotiated with the students. Self- and peer evaluations and teacher evaluations. Assessment is done *with* the students, not *to* the students.
A strategy checklist	See Appendix A for details. This checklist both reminds students of strategies they can try *and* encourages them to generate new ones.
Share sessions	See Table 2 for ideas.
Partnership and small-group work	Students share their thinking as they decide on, apply, and problem solve particular response strategies.
One-on-one conferences	The RRN facilitates these conferences and provides evidence of students' thinking.
Small-group discussions	Discussions become provisional and generative, leading to expanded thinking by participants.
Whole-class discussions	Teachers establish rigorous conditions. Discussions are speculative and students are able to revise their thinking.

Six Typical Challenges Children Encounter and Some Possible Solutions

In my years of experience using RRNs with children, the challenges that arise usually fit into one of the categories we use for assessment: *volume, variety, thoughtfulness,* or *maintenance.* Here are six typical challenges across these categories and some possible solutions. Some of these solutions we addressed in Chapter 4 but are worth summarizing here.

Volume: "I don't have enough time to write responses."	• Start with a one-on-one conference: what's challenging about finding time to write three entries/week? What the child reveals often leads to solutions. • Give reminders during each week: "How many entries have you written so far?" "It's Thursday. By now, you should have at least two entries this week." "Who needs to take home their RRN to complete one (or more) of your entries this week?" • Give reminders during reading workshop. Set a timer. "We have 10 minutes left. If you are planning to write an entry today, get started."
Variety: The child uses the same few strategies again and again.	• See the RRN Strategy Checklist (Appendix A; Chapter 4). • Share sessions, partnerships, and small-group work show students new possibilities (Chapter 4). • One-on-one conferences provide support to push students to try new strategies (Chapter 4).
Thoughtfulness: The child's responses seem superficial and lack purpose.	• Partnership, small-group, whole-class discussions and share sessions provide ample opportunities for students to experience thoughtful responses (Chapter 4). • One-on-one and small-group conferences provide support to push students to try strategies that meet or develop their reading purposes (Chapter 4). • Strategy lessons and reading workshop mini-lessons focusing on reader response strategies demonstrate matching purpose and choice for thoughtful responses (Chapters 2 and 3; see also especially "Strategies for Carving Out Time for Responding in Notebooks," p. 34).
Maintenance: The child's responses need proofreading and editing.	• Give reminders as students are wrapping up their responses: "Finish your thought. Read over what you wrote. Check for end punctuation. Check for capital letters. Check for any missing words. What can you do to make your writing easier to understand?" etc. • Teach students to check for high-frequency words (aka sight words, word wall words). Teach them to circle words they are unsure how to spell, try spelling each word another way in the margin, then write the word the best way above the way they wrote it. • Share sessions such as Pass the Notebook let students know that their responses will be shared with an audience, making spelling and punctuation matter more.
Maintenance: The child's work is messy.	• For some students, using a pen (instead of pencil) helps them to write more legibly: they don't need to press as hard for their writing to show up. • For writing in paragraph form, I instruct some students to skip lines. Skipping lines makes their writing more legible and provides more space for revising and proofreading. • Share sessions such as Pass the Notebook let students know that their responses will be shared with an audience, making overall neatness matter more.
Maintenance: The child has trouble managing her or his RRN.	• We try to involve parents as partners in using RRNs at home for homework. • Instead of having students store their notebooks in their desks, store them in bins that classroom helpers distribute and collect. • For some students, we keep their RRNs in school. We do not send their RRNs home for homework. They do their three responses per week in class only.

Permeable Boundaries: Living Literate Lives in and out of School

In Chapter 4, we established the sociocultural conditions that support our students as meaning makers in our classrooms. We believe it's imperative that our students gain proficiency with decoding and fluency and monitoring for sense; integrating semantic (meaning), syntactic, and graphophonic (visual) cues; and applying skill sets for deeper comprehension of texts. These skill sets include setting a purpose, making connections, predicting, asking questions, envisioning, inferring, determining importance, and drawing conclusions. In our classroom communities, learning to read strategically for deep comprehension is a process of learning to participate in textual interactions, and the language, tools, and practices of the RRN that we value are indicators of strategic reading. A key premise of sociocultural conditions is the connection of these practices of strategic reading to students' emerging identities. When we create classroom conditions that enable students to connect reading to who they are and want to be in the world, then they have desire, purpose, engagement, and motivation to develop proficiency with reading skills.

This chapter explores students' generative capacity as they reach Phase 3 in our gradual release of responsibility model (see Figure 11). They use RRNs to build connections between learning in and out of school, and we build these connections by inviting into the classroom popular culture and all manner of texts and encouraging students' inventiveness in responses, applying what Anne Haas Dyson (2003b) has called a "permeable curriculum." In the following sections, I showcase a broad range of student creativity, including responses to popular culture texts and to school-sanctioned texts using social media formats. I unpack what these entries demonstrate about students' deep comprehension of texts. Finally, I offer evidence of students using their notebooks for introspective journeys through texts rather than as retrospective accounts (Hancock, 1993).

TABLE 4. Students' Innovative RRN Responses

Type of Response	Explanation
Designing Social Media	• What would it be like if the main character had a Facebook or Instagram page? • What would the Twitter feeds sound like for this character? • What would a Google search bring up if we searched for this character online? • How would these characters sound if they texted each other about issues they are facing in the plot? These are just some of the explorations that students have pursued in their RRNs.
Designing Book Reviews	• What would a review on Amazon or Goodreads or Google+ sound like for this book, including comments from other people who read the review? • How would two friends use text messaging to discuss or recommend the book? These are just some of the ways that students have explored recommending texts they've read.
Drawing Character Relationships	Beyond a sketch-to-stretch (see Chapter 2) or character web of relationships (see Chapter 3), how else might we represent the relationships in the book that address central themes or issues that characters are contending with? How might we expand the use of sketch-to-stretch or character web of relationships for these purposes?
Drawing Pivotal Scenes or Plot Summaries or the Structural Workings of a Book	Students have used: • maps to trace a character's journey • comics to summarize key moments in the plot • representational drawing to imagine alternative endings

Generating Creative Responses

In the years that I have guided students in this work, across hundreds of notebooks, students continue to generate innovative responses to their reading for strategies we teach explicitly, as in Appendix C. But we also leave room for students to surprise us each year with their own creative responses to important texts in their lives. Table 4 lists *some* of the many creative responses students have generated, with a brief description of each. In the following sections, I continue to share more creative responses by students, based in strategies in Appendix C and Table 4.

Multigenre Responses

Multigenre writing is a set of strategies, based on the work of Tom Romano (2013), that we introduce explicitly to students (see Appendix C). Some scenes or cliffhanger moments in books cry out for alternative forms or genres of writing, and no author could ever provide all of these alternatives while remaining within the story world. How might a news reporter report on the events that just unfolded? If the ending were more conclusive, how would it go? How might a pivotal scene sound as a script (i.e., readers theater)? What would a journal entry by one of the characters sound like? What would one character say to another in a letter or a postcard or an e-mail? As Romano points out, the possibilities for multigenre responses are endless.

Romano (2013) provides several compelling reasons for the power and possibilities of multigenre writing. First, he explains how multigenre work harnesses students' imaginations, and "[w]hen we imagine, we see more deeply, we entertain possibilities we hadn't considered" (p. 11). Second, by responding in alternative forms and genres, students learn how those genres work and how voice in that genre might sound. This includes (a) the flexible use of language conventions, such as punctuation and syntax, that depends on form and genre; and (b) design and layout features of specific forms and genres. Multigenre writing offers opportunities to gain flexibility in a wide range of writing. Third, students are able to put themselves in characters' shoes, and by taking on characters' perspectives, they develop empathy and realize character complexity. Fourth, they develop author's craft. For example, by imagining an alternative ending or writing in a character's voice, they apply the author's writing style or the specific language and cadences of that character. Finally, they gain a truer sense of the expansive view of texts that we value for our RRN work. A narrative might be expressed as a song, a play, a news report, or a comic. Indeed, this variability is often what authors themselves do. Consider *J.T.*, by Jane Wagner (1972). It began as a ballad, then became a made-for-TV movie, and then became a bestselling children's book. *Coraline*, by Neil Gaiman (2012), is a novel, a graphic novel, and a stop-action animation movie. Both Wagner and Gaiman were active creators in the production of each of these texts.

Across their RRNs, students have used multigenre writing to:

- write alternative endings
- write a prologue or epilogue
- imagine journal entries from particular characters
- write letters from one character to another, or from themselves to a particular character or to the author
- imagine characters in the near or far-off future
- write a pivotal scene as a script
- write the plot as a ballad or found poem or as a comic strip
- write emails or postcards from a particular character to a specific audience of other characters

- write about a pivotal scene as a news report
- draw the setting as a map, a diagram, or a representational drawing
- write the book blurb for the back of the book
- write pretend interviews with key characters or with the author or illustrator

Not included in this list are the social media entries that I share in another section.

We've already seen some multigenre student work in previous chapters. I shared a few representational drawings, by Luiko (introduction, Figure 2), by Gabrielle (Figure 6), and by Henry (Figure 13). We saw Alyssa's comic strip of a pivotal scene in *The Graduation of Jake Moon* (Park, 2002; Figure 16b), as well as examples of found poems (Figures 27 and 28). All of these responses show deep inferential thinking, the ability to apply close reading for key details, character analysis, and envisionment.

Here are a few more examples that demonstrate the potential range of responses by elementary school students. In Figure 54, third grader Dylan imagined Philippe Petit's report card when he was an elementary school student, based on the personal traits he possessed in *The Man Who Walked between the Towers* (Gerstein, 2003). Dylan shows tremendous command of the school-based report card form, with the system, language, and categories of grading, the layout, the use of fonts, and distinguishing between categories that would receive numerical versus letter grades. Dylan also shows a playful awareness of Philippe's personality, such as scoring high marks in math but low grades in behavior. The teacher's comments acknowledge Philippe's academic abilities but also his challenging personal behavior. After all, Philippe had to be mischievous to successfully pull off tightrope walking across the Twin Towers.

Figure 55 is third grader Natalie's complete script of an alternative ending for *Ida B* (Hannigan, 2004). Like Dylan, Natalie demonstrates remarkable command of her chosen genre, scriptwriting. She begins with the cast of characters; notes each change of scene with passage of time; shows strong command of punctuation to meet her purposes, such as her use of ellipses, colons, parentheses, and exclamation marks; and uses all capital words to express

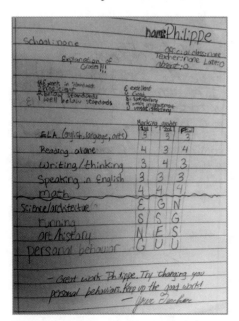

FIGURE 54. Philippe Petit's report card.

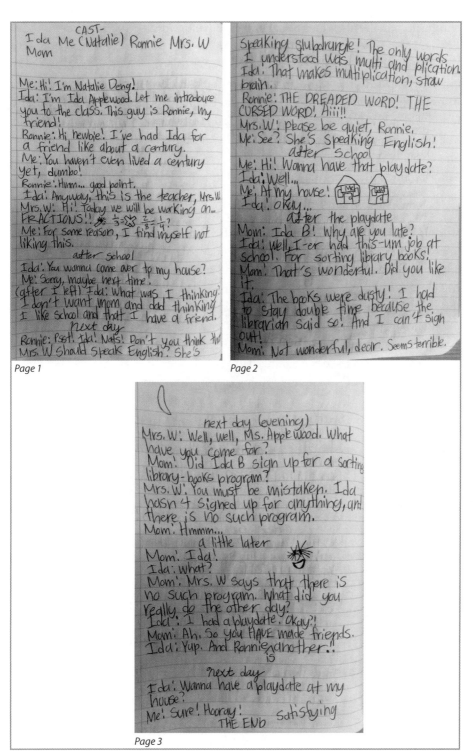

Page 1

Page 2

Page 3

FIGURE 55. The three-page script of an alternative ending to *Ida B.*

emphasis. Natalie also does notable work developing a script that flows like fan fiction. She addresses the central tension in *Ida B* of Ida B's contrarian and antisocial attitude toward school, expressing Ida B's tough, independent personality but also her kind inner core. She demonstrates a deep personal connection by inserting herself as the protagonist in the script who is able to befriend Ida B (and consequently ruin Ida B's guise of disliking school). The script has tension and a satisfying resolution. I also want to highlight Natalie's use of language. She creates dialogue that fits each character, that is funny, that flows, and that echoes Ida B's own language in the book. Natalie has clearly appropriated this language and "reverently reaccented" it for new purposes (Bakhtin, 1986).

Mid-year, Lauren Heinz and Debra Kessler's fourth-grade classes were studying the American Revolution. The RRN became a valuable tool for notetaking and thinking deeply about this history. Alex made the entries in Figures 56a and b. You can see key vocabulary and other parking lot notes, but the central focus is a letter from a patriot to his family. The letter captures the struggle of the fight against the British: the father's sense of despair, facing the pronounced imbalance of power, his enduring commitment to continue fighting even after being shot in the back, and ending the letter with the devastating declaration, "I think you'll never see me again." Through a letter format, Alex is able to put himself in the father's shoes, imagining his courage and hardship.

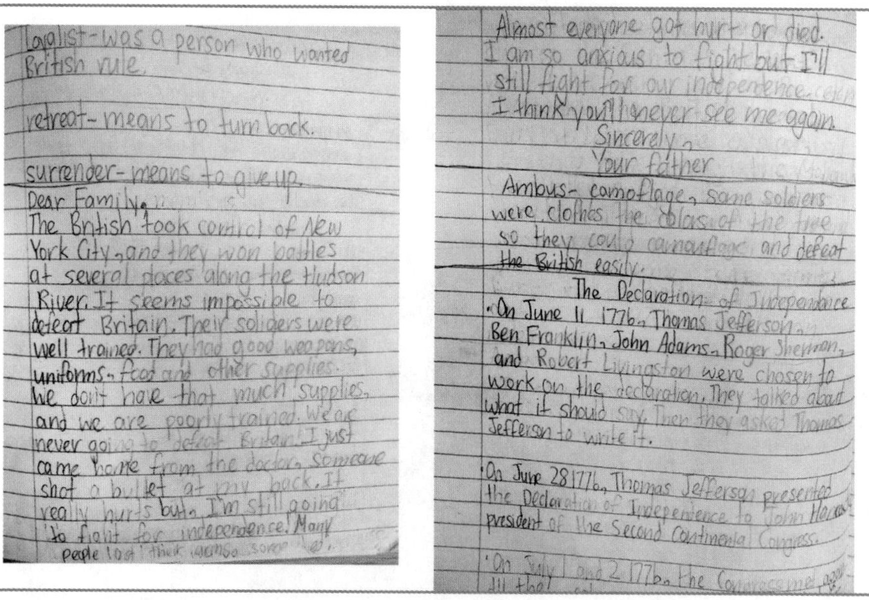
Loyalist-was a person who wanted British rule.

retreat-means to turn back.

surrender-means to give up.

Dear Family,
The British took control of New York City, and they won battles at several places along the Hudson River. It seems impossible to defeat Britain. Their soliders were well trained. They had good weapons, uniforms, food and other supplies. We don't have that much supplies, and we are poorly trained. We are never going to defeat Britain! I just came home from the doctor, someone shot a bullet at my back. It really hurts but, I'm still going to fight for independence! Many people lost

Almost everyone got hurt or died. I am so anxious to fight but I'll still fight for our independence. I think you'll never see me again.
Sincerely,
Your father

Ambus- camoflage, some soldiers were clothes the colors of the tree so they could camouflage and defeat the British easily.

The Declaration of Independence
• On June 11 1776, Thomas Jefferson, Ben Franklin, John Adams, Roger Sherman, and Robert Livingston were chosen to work on the declaration. They talked about what it should say. Then they asked Thomas Jefferson to write it.

• On June 28 1776, Thomas Jefferson presented the Declaration of Independence to John Hancock president of the Second Continental Congress.

• On July 1 and 2 1776, the Congressmen

FIGURE 56. A two-page letter home from a Revolutionary War patriot.

Edward, fifth grader, was reading *The Pushcart Wars* (Merrill & Solbert, 1964/2015). The title alone indicates a major power struggle, which is between the pushcart vendors and the big trucking companies that want to gain control of New York City streets. So it was entirely appropriate to imagine an interview by a reporter with Moe Mammoth, the owner of Mammoth Moving, one of the three trucking companies waging this war (see Figure 57). As in the previous examples, notice Edward's command of his genre, both in writing conventions and in voice. The reporter, for example, shows deference to "Mr. Moe" and uses questions and responses that get Mr. Moe to talk. Edward also appropriates Moe's bullying personality, which Edward rated at 95 percent on "The Evil Scale" in another entry. In the interview, Moe expresses his access to the mayor and his absolute justification for his own position and actions, saying, "I will order every truck to smash pushcarts. Hahaha!"

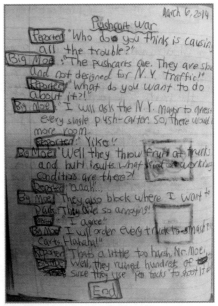

FIGURE 57. Moe's interview about *The Pushcart War.*

A final example is a news report by Adriana, also fifth grader. One of Lesley's read-aloud books was *The Graduation of Jake Moon* (Park, 2002), a harrowing story of how Jake and his family contend with his grandfather Skelly's deterioration from Alzheimer's disease. In one of the climactic episodes of the book, Skelly disappears for forty-eight hours, and then is found and brought safely home by a friendly taxi driver. It made so much sense for students to explore this episode in their RRNs. I shared Alyssa's comic book summary of this episode in Chapter 2, Figure 16b; Adriana was one of a few students who depicted it as a news report (see Figure 58). She presents the news report in the form of a comic strip involving a woman reporter behind a desk, a second anchor person (the man who thanks her for the report), plus the Good Samaritan taxi driver. The comic strip seems to be in a newspaper because Adriana includes two ads and "today's weather" at the bottom. So her response is a mash-up of two prominent genres. Like the other examples, Adriana's imaginative dialogic response shows command of these forms in language use, display, and overall design. The proficiency that all of

FIGURE 58. News report in comic form.

these students demonstrate is evidence of social and cultural learning of how these genres and forms work.

Recontextualizations

In Chapter 1, I explained Dyson's (2003a) use of the term *recontextualization* to indicate how children borrow and revoice familiar frames of reference, often based in popular culture texts, for new purposes. In the process, Dyson explains, they differentiate and expand their knowledge about and abilities with evolving communication practices. We can see recontextualization at work in the examples I've presented in this chapter, as students expressed deep comprehension about texts by playing around with diverse forms and genres of communication. Figures 3a and b in the introduction are also examples of recontextualizations. Figure 3a highlights Samantha's use of a coded message to reveal the motives of the protagonist, Eric, in *The Bully Book* (Gale, 2013); her message retains the same cryptic codes Eric receives and uses throughout the book to solve the mystery of the Bully Book that torments his life. In Figure 3b, Emma imagines a text message exchange between Mr. Collins, the seventh-grade math teacher in *All of the Above* (Pearsall, 2006), with his adult daughter at a pivotal moment in the story, right after the tetrahedron project with his afterschool math club was destroyed. In this section, I present work by fifth graders in Lesely Doff's class. Their entries play around with multigenre responses rooted in popular culture, including digital forms based in social media, that provide strong examples of recontextualization. What stands out are the *dialogic overtones* (Bakhtin, 1986) in these responses. It's often difficult to discern who is doing the talking in these responses, as if the students are having an internal dialogue with friends, with characters, with authors, with famous historical people. Let's take a look.

Figure 59 is a book review of *Because of Mr. Terupt* (Buyea, 2011) by Edward. As in all the preceding multigenre examples, Edward shows mastery of his chosen social form. He uses formal language and structure for the genre of a brief book review, providing examples to back up each claim, using transitional phrases to build coherence, and achieving a succinct summary of key plot events. Edward also shows mastery of the form of a social network site for book reviews. Notice the playful "interactive" ads at the top of the page, enticing users to "Buy Now!" or click on various links. He provides the URL for his "search," and his search of the key words "Mr. Terupt" found two results. He includes the thumbs up and thumbs down for likes and dislikes, as well as other format details, such as "comment hidden due to low rating." Edward uses punctuation and other language conventions flexibly as he plays in this imaginary social network site.

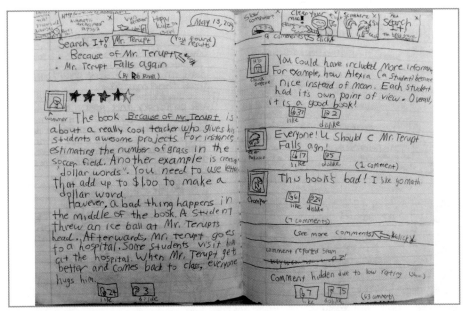

FIGURE 59. Book review of *Because of Mr. Terupt*.

For example, he knows that you can use texting shorthands, especially for comments ("Everyone! U should C Mr. Terupt Falls agn!"), and that viewers have monikers ("Chomper") and their own icons. By employing this social networking format for his review, Edward is able to be *multivoiced*: Chuck Greene comments on how to improve Edward's review; Peter Parkinson recommends the sequel; and Chomper expresses both dislike of the book and his preference for *Go Math,* a math program in New York City public schools that Edward's class disliked.

In Figure 60, Chloe depicts a pivotal scene early in the novel *Firegirl* (Abbott, 2008) using emojis. This is the scene when Jessica Feen, who has a disfigured face from being burned in a fire, is first introduced by the teacher, Mrs. Tracy, to the seventh-grade class at St. Catherine's Catholic School. The title of this entry, "Emojis in Real Life," indicates that Chloe is recontextualizing the superficial use of emojis, such as in text messages or as reactions to Facebook posts, for real life purposes. Chloe's layout of the emojis reveals the arrangement of individual desks in neat rows. She labels three key students, who are main

FIGURE 60. Emojis for *Firegirl*.

characters, and their distinctive reactions to Jessica's arrival, foreshadowing their actions toward Jessica once she joins the class. Chloe shows Mrs. Tracy holding Jessica's hand and looking at her students with a welcoming smile, but she uses a question mark for Jessica's face. An example of transmediation, the question mark is a metaphor for Jessica: Who is this disfigured girl? How did she get that way? How does she feel about facing this new group of classmates? How will they interact with one another? These are the central questions that propel the plot forward.

FIGURE 61. Tom texting with Jack.

In another entry, Chloe made a text-to-text connection of Tom in *Firegirl* to Jack in *Wonder* (Palacio, 2012). Both characters showed courage in befriending the disfigured protagonists, so Chloe imagined that naturally they would be friends. She designed an entry (Figure 61) in which Tom and Jack text message each other, illustrating how their texts would appear on each of their phones. In this exchange, she created a common story world in which the events in *Wonder* have already occurred, while the events in *Firegirl* are still unfolding, so Tom feels the need to reach out to Jack to share his angst, and Jack is able to offer advice ("Just cuz they look weird doesn't mean they're not a person"). Chloe shows such command of this social form of communication, using texting shorthands such as *ur, cuz,* and *G2G*; clipped exchanges, such as "Where?" "How?" "Ya"; speech bubbles and ellipses inside a speech bubble to indicate texting in progress. Through what seems like a simple form, Chloe is able to express the key central conflict that connects both these characters from two different novels.

Students also imagined how characters might use Facebook, Instagram, Twitter, or other social media if they had the opportunity. What would they post on their profiles? How many friends would they have? Who would be some of their friends? What kinds of news posts would they make? What kinds of comments would they receive? What images might they share? In Figure 62, Serena imagines a Facebook post by Prudence Galewski from the historical novel *Deadly* (Chibbaro & Sovak, 2012). *Deadly* takes place in 1909 in New York City and vicinity, as health officials try to solve a medical mystery and prevent an outbreak of typhoid, a

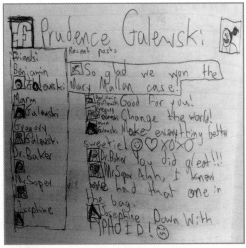

FIGURE 62. Facebook page for *Deadly*'s Prudence Galewski.

deadly disease. Prudence is fortunate to become an assistant to Mr. Soper as they work tirelessly to solve the case, eventually tracking down the carrier of the disease, Mary Mallon (aka Typhoid Mary). Serena's response imagines Prudence's Facebook post after solving the case and the responses it might receive from her Facebook friends. These friends offer appropriate comments on Prudence's post based on their character relationships to her in the story. For example, it makes sense that Marm Galewski, Prudence's mother, would call her "Sweetie" and use icons such as a smiley face, a heart, and hugs and kisses, or that Mr. Soper would use the inclusive *we,* since they worked together as a team, or that Dr. Baker would encourage her, as he recognized her analytic abilities in the story and encouraged her to study medicine.

The final example of recontextualization is Ken's design of playing cards for Greek gods (see Figure 63). Ken read a lot of Greek mythology and loved the Percy Jackson and the Olympians series. He designed the playing cards in a format similar to Pokémon or Magic: The Gathering cards. The top of each card names the Greek god and his or her power points. Zeus and Poseidon are both high-power gods, worth 800 points, whereas Hades is worth 500 power points. Then comes a picture of the god in his or her natural setting. Hades, for example, is floating on his boat on the River Styx. Next, Ken reveals the god type: Thunder type no. 1; Dead type no. 2; Water type no. 3. The next panel shows the relative values of the gods' power attributes. For example, Poseidon is adept at swordplay, which is valued at 200 points. Finally, the bottom panel gives key descriptors of each god. For example, Ken writes, "Zeus is the king of Greek gods. He is the thunder god. He is married to Hera." What a wonderful way to catalog

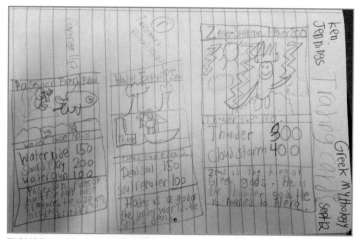

FIGURE 63. Playing cards for Greek gods.

the Greek gods that Ken was studying! It makes so much sense to have these kind of playing cards for Greek gods. And, in case they haven't yet been marketed, Ken provides copyright and trademark numbers for his design.

Across all of these examples, it's clear that by enabling the interplay of a permeable curriculum that allows students to utilize multiple genres and forms in their nonschool worlds, their deep thinking about school-sanctioned texts is enriched.

Reformulations, Revisited

In Chapter 3, I introduced reformulations, and we explored examples from Lauren Heinz's fourth-grade class using *Cactus Hotel* (Guiberson & Lloyd, 1991) and *Desert Giant* (Bash, 1989). Figure 3c in the introduction is also an example of reformulation, depicting a map of the route that Skelly, who has Alzheimer's, took through the town on the night he wandered away from home unattended, in *The Graduation of Jake Moon* (Park, 2002). Reformulation responses are the epitome of close reading—the kind of analytical reading that state and national standards value. The Partnership for Assessment of Readiness for College and Careers (PARCC) provides a useful definition for teaching with these standards in mind:

> Close, analytic reading stresses engaging with a text of sufficient complexity directly and examining meaning thoroughly and methodically, encouraging students to read and reread deliberately. Directing student attention on the text itself empowers students to understand the central ideas and key supporting details. It also enables students to reflect on the meanings of individual words and sentences; the order in which sentences unfold; and the development of ideas over the course of the text, which ultimately leads students to arrive at an understanding of the text as a whole. (2011, p. 7)

Throughout the year, students continue to use this strategy and invent new forms for important texts in their lives. As they do, we experience students' embodiments of this kind of close, analytical reading: scanning, rereading, highlighting, underlining, coding, and writing marginal notes. Here is a partial list of reformulations that students have explored:

- timelines of events

- charts for character analysis, animal attributes, accumulating information, and so on

- T-charts, H-charts, double bubble maps, and Venn diagrams for comparisons

- webs for mapping out conceptual understandings and relationships

- maps

- diagrams

- thinking maps: flow maps, double bubble maps, tree maps, and so on

- mathematical representations, such as line graphs, bar graphs, pie graphs, percentages, analytical charts, and various numerical equations

Let's take a look at a few of these and what they reveal of students' deep comprehension.

In Figure 64, fourth grader Caitlin uses a web to conceptually lay out all the causes and effects of the American Revolution, which students were studying in social studies. The web shows a synthesis of information across multiple texts. Caitlin color-coded lines to demarcate groups and policies and causes of key events. She wrote in the genre of note-taking, using abbreviations (e.g., G.W.), phrases, and sentence fragments. Her web is laden with key vocabulary for this topic, such as *Minute Men, Sons of Liberty, colonies, parliament,* and *independence*. Notice as well her attention to language conventions, such as capitalization and the use of ellipses, the ampersand, and periods for abbreviations.

In Figure 65a, fifth grader Eric plots August's journey in *Wonder* (Palacio, 2012). With a positive to negative y-axis, the line graph depicts both key events and August's emotional journey. Eric's graph

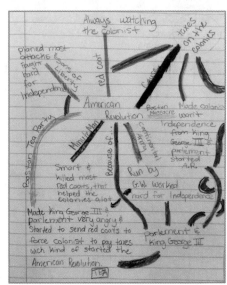

FIGURE 64. Caitlin's American Revolution web.

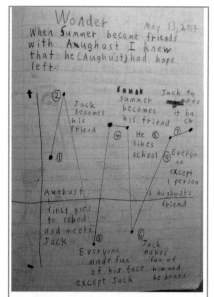

(a) Eric's plot for August in Wonder.

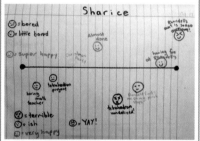

(b) Kristina's plot for Sharice in All of the Above.

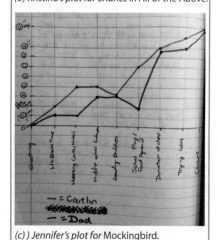

(c)) Jennifer's plot for Mockingbird.

FIGURE 65. Examples of students' plot diagrams for novels.

shows his grasp of x,y-coordinate graphing, such as understanding positive and negative and temporal dimensions. In addition, the graph demonstrates his narrative understanding that central characters experience both external action and internal emotional journeys that result in character development and change. In Figure 65b, Kristina uses emoticons to do similar work, showing the emotional journey of Sharice at key plot points in *All of the Above* (Pearsall, 2006). The emoticons are also color coded for further emphasis. Kristina's graph hints at an x- and a y-axis by placing the emoticons in sequential order above or below the horizontal line with finite end points, thereby also demonstrating her knowledge of graphing skills. Some students used x,y-coordinate graphing to compare characters' internal journeys and resolutions of conflicts. In Figure 65c, Jennifer plots both Caitlin and her dad's emotional journeys as they pursue closure after the school shooting death of Caitlin's older brother, Devon, in the book *Mockingbird* (Erskine, 2011). Plotting both Caitlin and her dad's internal conflicts together makes a lot of sense since the novel contends with both of their journeys from despair to reconciliation. Jennifer's graph reminds us that line graphs are an excellent way to show comparisons.

Students make diagrams of all kinds in their RRNs. We see diagrams of animals, of body parts, of plants (as we saw for the saguaro cactus in Chapter 3), of planets and outer space, of specific places. Diagrams are so useful for depicting parts of a whole, and coupled with labels and descriptions, they provide a comprehensive view of a topic. Fourth grader Nicholas loved reading about human anatomy. (Perhaps he'll grow up to be a medical doctor or researcher?) How wonderful to enable students to pursue passions and interests in their classroom reading! He drew diagrams of the brain, the skeletal system, and the digestive system, and included key information he had discovered for each one. Figure 66 is his diagram of the heart. The title indicates that this is his "Human Body Drawing

#18." He uses arrows and color coding to show the flow of blood through major valves and the color pink to demarcate the major sections of the heart. Nicholas also clearly has a sense of audience that determines his authoritative voice in this entry: the diagram teaches. He addresses his audience directly, even academically, including a "Did you know" panel.

Students also pursued mathematical responses, which illustrate excellent strategies for thinking through events, exploring character traits and relationships, or working like detectives to solve mysteries. Like the plot graphs, these graphic representations provide a strong basis of comparison to sort through key details. In Figure 67a, fourth grader Yasmin used a bar graph to compare the lengths of different snakes she had read about. In Figure 67b, fifth grader Jennifer used a pie chart to explore what was

FIGURE 66. Nicholas's heart diagram.

important to James Harris III, one of the central characters, at the beginning of *All of the Above* (Pearsall, 2006). She drew new pie charts for James as a basis of comparison for the middle and end of the book. In Figure 67c, fourth grader Matthew used vectors to explore percentages of important skills for key characters in *The Sign of the Beaver* (Speare, 1983). In Figure 67d, fifth grader Devin used a chart to analyze key components of the "grunts," or the characters who are being bullied, in *The Bully Book* (Gale, 2013), as he sorted out the mystery of who is behind The Bully Book. As with the x,y-coordinate graphs, each of these responses also reveals what each student understands about the mathematical concepts of these ways of representing information. For example, notice how Yasmin labeled both the vertical and the horizontal axes, provided a graph title, indicated feet in even intervals of two, and was able to show lengths that fall between the even intervals.

Students have created these and so many more creative reformulations to explore their thinking for deep comprehension of important texts in their lives. The final example I'll present is second grader Tyler's T-chart (Figures 68a and b) for *Diary of a Wimpy Kid: The Long Haul* (Kinney, 2014). Tyler analyzes Greg's facial expressions, using red and blue to demarcate two common ones; in fact, the blue facial expression is from the book cover. He's aware that in graphic novels inferring characters' emotional states requires analyzing both the words and the drawings. As you can see in Figure 68b, Tyler marked this entry with sticky

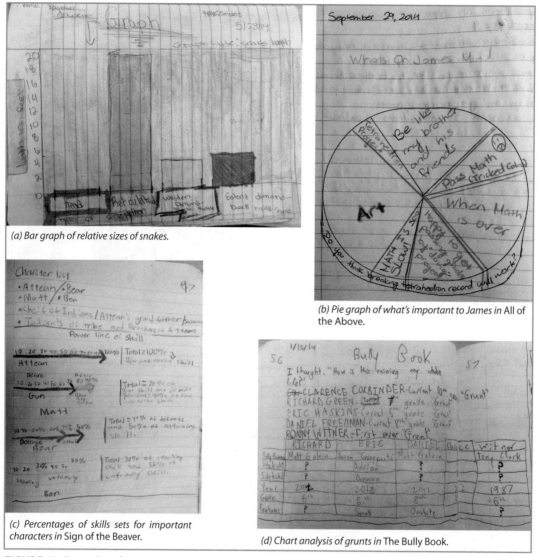

(a) Bar graph of relative sizes of snakes.

(b) Pie graph of what's important to James in All of the Above.

(c) Percentages of skills sets for important characters in Sign of the Beaver.

(d) Chart analysis of grunts in The Bully Book.

FIGURE 67. Examples of mathematical responses in RRNs.

notes as one of his favorites for his ability to infer Greg's feelings by reading his face. Also notice Tyler's correct use of parentheses and of capital letters for the book title.

In Chapter 1, I shared Romano's (2013) lament: "The [s]tandards want writing that's all head, no heart" (p. 189). As in the section on reformulations in Chapter 3, the examples I've shared here are proof that even close, analytical reading—the kind of thinking that state and national standards value—doesn't

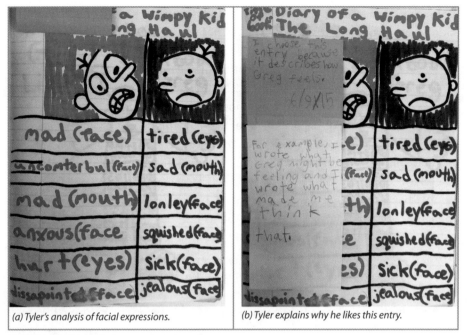

(a) Tyler's analysis of facial expressions.

(b) Tyler explains why he likes this entry.

FIGURE 68. Tyler's T-chart and explanation.

need to be all head and no heart (even when Nicholas creates a response about the heart). Analytical thinking should and needs to include elements of design: layout, use of color, special fonts, visual display. Coupled with language, design becomes part of the students' meaning-making process (Albers, 2007; Eisner, 1998; Leigh, 2010). These examples, then, defy the various standards' "verbo-centric" emphasis in school-based responses (Siegel, 2006) that contends that the only way for students to show deep comprehension is through written work.

Permeable Boundaries

In the "Recontextualizations" section, we saw a permeable curriculum at work. Dyson (2003a) contends: "It is the processes of transporting and transforming material across symbolic and social borders—and the interplay of childhoods and school agendas they entail—that are at the heart of the developmental vision" (p. 10) for students. In this section, I present examples of students' analytical responses to popular culture texts. I've shared several examples already in previous chapters. In Chapter 2, I shared students' ongoing lists that embraced popular culture, such as Wissal's "Favorite Movies" (Figure 20b) and Michael's "Favorite NFL Teams" (Figure 20c). In fact, most of students' ongoing lists embraced popular culture interests, such as "Favorite Txting Terms," "Favorite Video Games," or "Favorite Songs." In Chapter 3, I shared Miguel's character list and web of relationships for *Sponge Bob Square Pants* (Figure 25). In Figure 32, I shared Terrence's analysis of a wolf in the virtual world of Minecraft, from *Minecraft: Essential Handbook* (Milton, 2014). His design shows key attributes, such as drops, where it is found, and hostility level. In addition to these terms, Terrence uses other sophisticated vocabulary of this world, such as *experience orbs, grassy areas, forests, taiga, biomes, hostility, hostile, neutral,* and *attacked.* His visual display shows understanding of diagrams, including arrows and labels, text boxes, icons, and colons for categories.

In Chapter 1, citing Dolby (2003) and Dyson (2003b), I stated: "Students engage in social affiliations that form their identities through agentive actions with popular culture, and these actions are inherently educational." My aim now is to show what I also stated in Chapter 1: that students do similar interpretive work for all texts if we provide opportunities—in other words, if we create permeable boundaries.

Let's first look at Eisuke's response to "GO Galaxy" in Figure 69. Eisuke was a fifth grader, bilingual in Japanese and English, and loved Japanese anime. One of his favorite anime series was Lightning Eleven GO Galaxy, an all-star youth soccer team that in the story will represent Japan at the Youth International Soccer World Championship. Eisuke used his notebook to think through the roster and character relationships. On the top of the page, he wrote the title, "Lightning Eleven Go Galaxy," in both English and Japanese. He provided three related responses on this page. On the left side, he listed the players, using symbols for gender (♀, ♂) and soccer positions (e.g., GK = Goal Keeper; DF = Defense; FW = Forward). As with the title, Eisuke wrote players' names in both English and Japanese. Next to their names he gave letters for order of importance to the team. On the right, Eisuke showed the team formation using the designated letters for each player, including two substitute players (M and L). In the character web of relationships at the bottom of the page, he placed Tenma, the team captain, in the center. He color-coded and grouped players who have strong affiliations with one another and based on the positions they play. A black circle brings all the players together as a team, led by the coach, Kuroiwa, also written in black. This entry also showcases Eisuke's use of visual display—layout, draw-

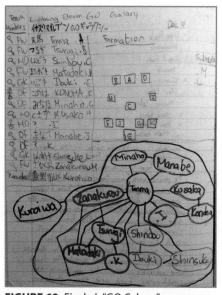

FIGURE 69. Eisuke's "GO Galaxy" responses.

ing tools, color, and other design elements—as a semiotic resource to express and explore meaningful texts in his life.

In Figures 70a and b, Luke made a multigenre response, turning into a script his experience of meeting, along with his older brother, Scott, with his rabbi about the Torah portions for their bar mitzvahs. As with other multigenre examples I've shared, Luke shows strong command of his chosen genre of writing. He correctly applies the conventions for scriptwriting, such as assigning speaking roles, offsetting each turn with colons, indicating passages of time in parentheses, using all capital letters for emphasis, and stretching out words to match how a person should say them. He designs the title, "My Torah Portion," to look like a Torah scroll, and shows excellent command of punctuation, such as "PLEEEAASE?!?" His script expresses his sense of humor and attitude toward his religious training, such as spinning in the swivel chair and hearing what the rabbi describes about his brother's Torah portion as BLAH BLAH BLAH BLAH BLAH. His interactions with the rabbi are both playful and respectful. Luke also applies the dramatic arc of a skit, starting with small talk about recent movies with the rabbi, then discussing their Torah portions, and concluding with leaving with their parents for dinner at Uno's. Luke's entry demonstrates his capacity to use a script to negotiate and express his social and cultural experiences.

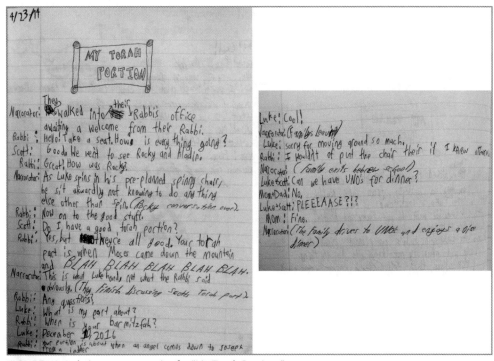

FIGURE 70. Luke's two-page script for "My Torah Portion."

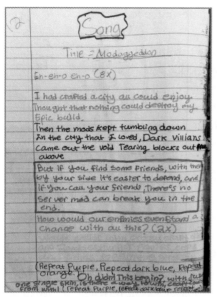

FIGURE 71. Song lyrics for "Modageddon."

In Figure 71, fourth grader Dyandra uses color coding for each verse and chorus of the song "Modageddon," a parody of "Pompeii," by the band Bastille. Dyandra didn't simply copy the lyrics. Her entry shows her strong structural analysis of the song: (1) she underlines and centers the title; (2) she starts with the repeated chant in its own color (eh-eh-o eh-o); (3) she gives each verse its own color; (4) she draws a red box around the chorus; (5) she gives directions in parentheses for how to sing each part; and (6) she starts each verse on a new line and begins with a capital letter. She also pays attention to spelling and other punctuation, such as commas and questions marks. Dyandra's analysis of text structure for this song shows great promise for transfer of understanding text structure to other songs and similar genres, such as poetry.

In Figures 72a and b, third grader Sandra performs character analysis in chart format, a rather typical form of response for school. What is different with this response is that (a) Sandra did it entirely on her own, without prompting; (b) she did it for her own purpose of thinking about the text, not to please the teacher; and (c) she was responding to an animated movie she had seen recently, *Epic*, about a teenage girl, Mary Katherine (aka M.K.), who is thrust into the middle of a battle of good versus evil to save a forest. Notice all the conventions of language that Sandra applies for chart writing, including sketches of the characters; labels and commentary; use of parentheses, possessives, and contractions; and use of key words, phrases, and sentence fragments for note-taking.

I include these entries to emphasize my point that all students can do similar deep interpretive work of any texts that matter to them—if we create permeable boundaries for this work.

My final examples illustrating the importance of permeable boundaries are two entries, one by third grader Thomas (Figure 73a) and one by fifth grader Eisuke (Figure 73b), in response to texts that matter in their lives. Both report on the texts they engaged with during spring vacation. For Thomas it was playing pool, and for Eisuke it was practicing piano music. Both students realize that these are activities that require skill, insight, and application of strategies. In other words, if these are activities that matter in their lives, then they are worthy of response. Thomas chose to respond by creating a Facebook post that he marked "This page is really cool!" As a third grader, Thomas imagines that this is the kind of activity Facebook users might post, and he explores what the

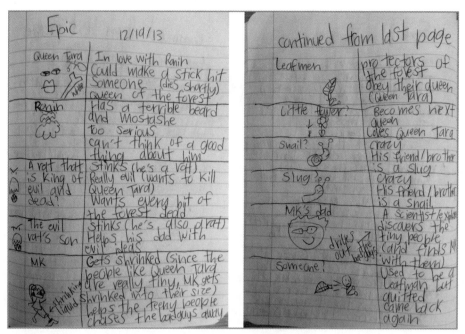

FIGURE 72. Sandra's two-page character analysis for *Epic*.

design of this kind of post might look like. He starts with the Facebook logo and then deliberately uses language that he imagines is appropriate for a Facebook post, such as *bro, lol,* and the smiley face emoticon. He includes a drawing of a pool table that in a real Facebook post might be a photo. In addition to assigning a different color to demarcate each statement, he uses appropriate language and length for a Facebook audience. His cross-outs show his attention to spelling, and he demonstrates understanding of colons, capitalization, and exclamation marks. Eisuke knows that music is another important form of reading. His letters on the right-hand side show how to decode the notes for both treble and bass clefs. He also uses colors deliberately to support decoding. For example, on the treble clef all A notes are brown, all E notes are blue, and all B notes are pink. He explains his purpose: if he does well on the piano test, he can go to a good music school.

How might we connect Thomas's or Eisuke's personal interests with the school curriculum? In other words, if we create permeable boundaries, how might we build bridges between home and school? A few ideas come to mind, and I'm sure you can think of others. In their school writing, both Thomas and Eisuke might choose the topics they've explored in these responses. In math, when we study vectors or two-dimensional geometry, I might build connections to playing pool, or when we study fractions, I might build connections to read-

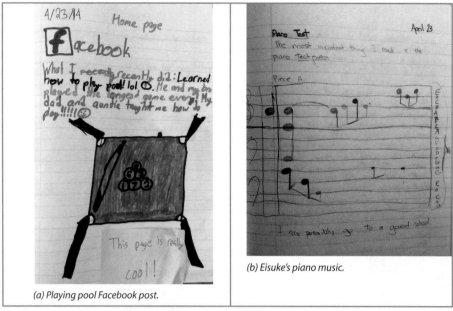

(a) Playing pool Facebook post.

(b) Eisuke's piano music.

FIGURE 73. Examples of students' RRN entries about texts that matter in their lives.

ing musical notes. I might bring up motion and collision of pool balls or the science of sound when we study physical science. I might support these students in building text sets around these topics that they could explore for independent reading or when we visit the school library. I might connect them with online sites and apps for further exploration.

As I explained in Chapter 3, according to Freebody and Luke (1990), literate people express four dimensions: they are code breakers, meaning makers, text users, and text critics. Thomas's and Eisuke's responses show their abilities as code breakers, meaning makers, and text users. They decoded the components of playing pool, posting on Facebook, and reading music; they derived meaning from these activities; and they know how to access and engage with these activities in purposeful ways. Their responses highlight how they are becoming literate people. In the next section, I explore students' responses as text critics.

Critical Literacy Responses

Freebody and Luke (1990) explain that text critics are able to analyze and critique texts around issues of power, perspective, and social justice. They recognize how texts position them as readers and determine whether to accept or take an oppositional stance, based on which subjectivities they suppress or express. Appendix C shows some of the critical literacy responses we explicitly taught students. All the responses in which students take on particular characters' perspectives, consistent with multigenre writing, are examples of critical literacy responses. In these responses, students showed remarkable capacity for empathy, taking on perspectives as varied as a Confederate soldier who supports slavery, an old man who is suffering from Alzheimer's disease, a grandmother who doesn't have enough money to buy her grandson fancy new sneakers, a big brother who is forced to fill in the town swimming pool with tar to prevent people like himself and his younger brother from swimming there, a tightrope walker who walks between the Twin Towers. In this section, I share a few strategies students used to do critical readings of texts: digging deeper, leaning in, dialogic responses, mind/alternative mind, power meters, narrative switch, and persuasive letters.

Digging Deeper and Leaning In

Two other strategies we taught students to envision the story world or to infer deeply about characters were *digging deeper* and *leaning in* from *Notebook Connections* by Aimee Buckner (2009). Both of these strategies helped students to step into characters' shoes and see the story world from their perspectives. In leaning in, students identify a pivotal scene and write descriptively, imagining a central character's sensory experiences. In digging deeper, students imagine the central character's thoughts and feelings.

Figures 74a and b are examples of these two strategies. After reading *The Big Bug Book* (Facklam & Facklam, 1994), third grader Natalie was amazed by the tarantula hawk wasp: how it battles the tarantula in order to provide food for its larvae. She decided to lean in to imagine this battle. Natalie's response is not a simple rewording of the page in the book that describes this battle. For one thing, she got some facts wrong. She states that the wasp bites the tarantula, when the passage states that the wasp uses its stinger. She indicates that the larvae hatch after three years, when in fact the passage states that they hatch after two or three days. She also states that the tarantula is dead when the larvae eat it, when in fact the passage tells us that the tarantula is alive but paralyzed from the wasp's venom, so it's basically eaten alive. But Natalie's description also provides more perspectives than the passage does. For example, the passage states:

When the wasp and spider meet, the spider rears up on four hind legs, ready for battle. The wasp hovers overhead, darting in and out until she sees her chance to plunge her stinger into the tarantula. The wasp's venom puts the spider's muscles out of action. It cannot move, but it is not dead. (p. 18)

Natalie describes the battle as follows. (Note: I put content-specific words and phrases that Natalie uses from the passage in *italic.*)

Just as she spots one, that one spots her. It *rears up* to attack and charges the wasp. But the wasp quickly *hovers* above the tarantula and looks for a good spot to bite and insert *venom* into the tarantula. The spider suddenly opens it's mouth, baring its fangs. The wasp dives in the tarantula body and bites. The tarantula freezes and stops moving. Its eyes glare at the wasp, but it is helpless.

Natalie uses background knowledge to imagine more of the spider's active role in the battle, such as charging the wasp or opening its mouth to bare its fangs. Her rewording also shows her understanding of key concepts. All told, Natalie is able to envision this harrowing scene and imagine the perspectives of the wasp, the tarantula, and the "wasp babies."

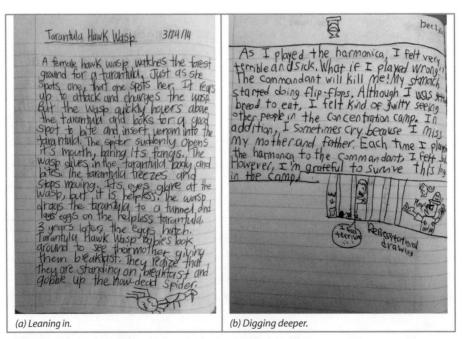

(a) Leaning in.

(b) Digging deeper.

FIGURE 74. Examples of leaning in and digging deeper strategies.

In Figure 74b, fifth grader Michael uses digging deeper to infer the harrowing experience of the Jewish narrator of *The Harmonica* (Johnston & Mazellan, 2004). This picture storybook takes place in Europe during World War II. The narrator and his parents are sent to separate concentration camps and only he survives. The story is about how the harmonica saves him and provides hope to other prisoners. Michael is able to imagine the narrator's thoughts and feelings: his panic about playing for the commandant, his guilt about being rewarded bread when other prisoners are starving, his yearning for his parents. Michael's representational drawing reinforces his description, showing the narrator's worried face with the label "I feel terrible . . ." He reinforces the commandant as a "bad guy." The animal might represent the German shepherds who are depicted in the picture book at the commandant's feet when the boy plays for him. The drawing also shows some of Michael's misconceptions, such as the boy, attached to a ball and chain, behind bars. Ultimately, Michael's entry demonstrates his ability to take on the narrator's perspective to imagine the horrific world of this story.

Dialogic Responses

We also saw incredible examples of students' capacities to imagine multiple perspectives in their multivoiced, *dialogic responses*. Earlier in this chapter, I discussed and shared examples of letter writing (see Figure 56), text messaging, scripts (see Figure 55), mock interviews (see Figure 57), and social network responses that included comments from viewers (see Figure 59). In these dialogic responses, characters within the same text or across texts spoke to each other (see Figure 61), students spoke directly with characters or the author (see Figure 75a), or students invented reporters as proxies to speak with them (see Figure 58).

We saw this capacity to take on multiple perspectives even from second graders. Figures 75a and b are examples from Morgan, who, after reading the picture book *The Man Who Walked between the Towers* (Gerstein, 2003), decided to write directly to Philippe Petit, the tightrope walker who walked across the Twin Towers without permission on August 7, 1974, before they were officially open to the public. In Morgan's letter to Philippe, he scolds Philippe for doing something so dangerous, especially when he knew that it was illegal. He even addresses Philippe as "Crazy Philippe" and closes his letter with "make better choices." What's especially delightful is that in Morgan's next entry, Philippe writes back to him. As you read it, ask yourself: Who's doing the talking in this letter? Is it Morgan? Or is it Philippe? Morgan expresses Philippe's voice in playful ways, responding to Morgan's questions and concerns. Philippe acknowledges that

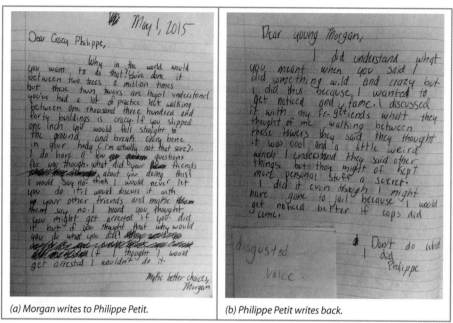

(a) Morgan writes to Philippe Petit. (b) Philippe Petit writes back.

FIGURE 75. Letter "exchange" between Morgan and Philippe Petit.

his friends thought his plan was "a little weird" and that "they might of kept more personal stuff a secret." He addresses the letter to "young Morgan" and also gives advice in his closing, "Don't do what I did." Morgan even includes a sticky note advising the reader to read Philippe's response in a "disgusted voice." Notice as well the evidence of proofreading, with all the cross-outs and the use of a caret to insert a missing word. All told, Morgan expresses his capacity for realizing multiple perspectives by both challenging a protagonist in a text and having the protagonist challenge right back.

Mind/Alternative Mind

Another strategy we taught students to help them perceive multiple perspectives is *mind/alternative mind*, a strategy we learned from Maureen McLaughlin and Glen DeVoogd's *Critical Literacy* (2004). In this strategy, students draw two faces opposing each other on the same page to represent opposing points of view in the same text or from two different texts. Here are two examples from Lesley Doff's fifth-grade class. In Figure 76a, Stephen uses this strategy to represent the thoughts and feelings of one of the "grunts" (a kid who is the target of bullying) and one of the bullies in *The Bully Book* (Gale, 2013). Lesley taught her students to include feelings, emotions, questions, and statements in their mind/

alternative mind responses. Stephen also shows distinctions in his drawings. William, the grunt, looks forlorn. He has furrowed brows and cheeks and a dour mouth. His eyes are askance, as if he's nervously looking around for where the next torment will come from. One of his thoughts is about suicide. Tony, on the other hand, has a broad, toothy grin, with closed eyes, facing straight ahead, to express his confident delight in his position of power as one of the bullies. It's so appropriate that Stephen opens up their skulls to reveal their brains and draws lines from the yellow spots that represent their thoughts and feelings. The sticky note shows that Stephen chose this entry as one of his favorites because "I expressed my thoughts through pictures of the people and the brain."

In Figure 76b, Jonah drew mind/alternative mind for the protagonist and the tormentor in two highly comparable books, *Firegirl* (Abbott, 2008) and *Wonder* (Palacio, 2012). So this drawing provides alternative perspectives for four main characters while making text-to-text connections. Jonah quite appropriately drew the characters as faceless cutouts, just as the authors of both books intended, leaving what they looked like up to readers' imaginations. Jonah was also deliberate in his choice of colors. He drew both tormentors in yellow, which vibrates with energy that these characters exude. Jessica, in *Firegirl*, who was disfigured by fire, is represented in red, which also might convey her rage at what happened to her. August, in *Wonder*, is represented by blue, which con-

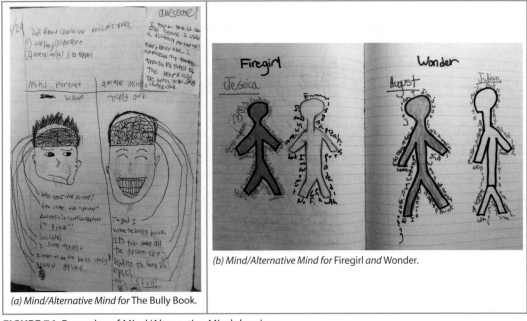

(a) *Mind/Alternative Mind for* The Bully Book.

(b) *Mind/Alternative Mind for* Firegirl *and* Wonder.

FIGURE 76. Examples of Mind/Alternative Mind drawings.

veys calm and wisdom and sincerity. Jonah then outlines each silhouette with their thoughts and feelings, managing to convey both the hurt and anger of Jessica's and August's victimization and the disgust and jealousy of Jeff and Julian. (Note: I transcribed words I couldn't decipher as [?].) For Jessica: "I hate my mom. Stupid Tom going with stupid Jeff. Everyone is mean to me. I HATE JEFF! I won't ever be the same. I'll always be after [?] FIRE." For Jeff: "Ewww is she a freak. Stupid Tom with his G. F. [girlfriend]. No time for me. I don't care. Why should I?" For August: "I'm just like a normal kid. What do they think of me? [?] I do [?]? I wanna go home. Who cares about Julian?" For Julian: "Get out of our school [?]. Jack is with the freak. Why is Jack with him. Auggie ruined everything. Stupid."

An imperative dimension of critical readings is analyzing how various characters are positioned, who has power, and how power is wielded in the story world (and in life). Power and positioning in the story world, just like in real life, are dynamic and contextual. In what contexts in your own life do you feel competent and confident? How about inept and withdrawn? An integral part of developing confidence and competency is how well a context considers and accommodates our needs and wants. For me, I feel competent and confident on the tennis court or as a presenter for topics in literacy. I feel inept and withdrawn among a team of mechanics in an airplane hangar or among strangers in a boisterous bar scene. When we gain agency and competence—or, put another way, when we gain more power—we might use that power for good or bad purposes. I gain confidence as a literacy coach each time I'm able to help school faculty problem solve and improve their practices. I work hard to use my power for good purposes by building on their strengths and helping them grow in their competencies. It's what good teachers do every day.

Power Meter

One way we teach students to realize these dynamics in texts they read is with a strategy I call a *power meter*. In a power meter, students are able to show how much power one character or multiple characters have at a particular plot point. Some students have drawn power meters at different points in a book as a basis for exploring character change and development. How students represent a power meter is up to them, and for some students, their depictions take on dimensions of sketch-to-stretch when the representation also serves as a metaphor for deeper meanings. Figures 77a and b are examples for *Freedom Summer* (Wiles & Lagarrigue, 2001) from two students in Deb Kessler's fourth-grade class. Figure 77c is a power meter for Willy Q, a character in *All of the Above* (Pearsall, 2006).

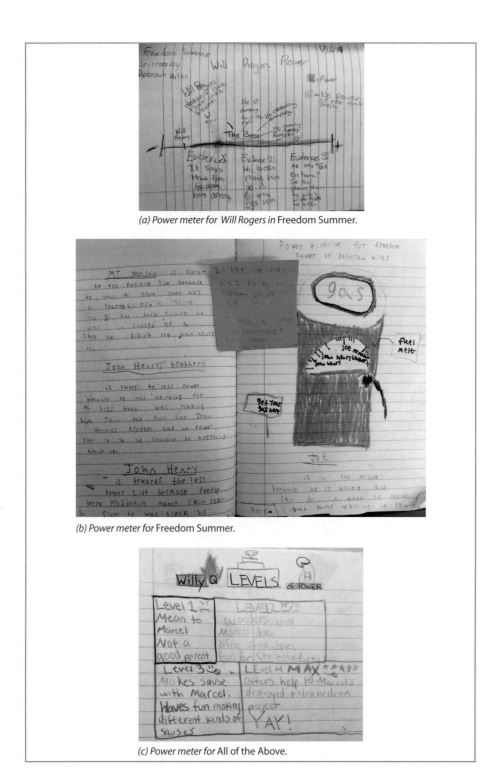

(a) Power meter for *Will Rogers* in Freedom Summer.

(b) Power meter for Freedom Summer.

(c) Power meter for All of the Above.

FIGURE 77. Examples of students' power meter drawings.

In Figure 77a, Reyna focuses on Will Rogers's power in *Freedom Summer*. Will Rogers is a secondary character, the older brother of one of the protagonists, John Henry. Will Rogers appears in one pivotal scene as one of the workers who fills the town pool with tar to prevent "Colored People" from swimming there, right after town officials allow integration. Reyna's power meter includes several design features that allow her to compare Will Rogers's power to that of the work crew boss. She provides a key that shows pink for power and blue for "no power or not that much." She uses a line scale that marks blue negative (-) to pink positive (+) range, and identifies where on this scale Will Rogers and the boss are. Above the scale, Reyna provides three reasons why the boss has the power. This is evidence of her close, analytical reading because the book never focuses on the boss; readers are left entirely on their own to infer about the boss from context clues. Below the line, Reyna provides three pieces of evidence from the book that support why she marked Will Rogers with low power and concluded that "Will Rogers doesn't have that much power." Reyna also appropriately titled and dated her entry.

Conversely, Giancarlo uses a power meter to compare four central characters in *Freedom Summer* (see Figure 77b). He does a number of interesting things in his design. He provides explanations for how much power each of these characters has. His reasons show his emerging understanding of how people access power for good or bad purposes (e.g., part of Mr. Mason's power is that he didn't let John Henry into his store) that are based on race (e.g., the relative positions of power for John Henry and Joe because of the color or their skins), on socioeconomic class (e.g., Will Rogers is forced to work for a boss), and on whether you are a child or an adult (e.g., there's nothing Joe can do to help the situation because he's still a kid). Equally important is Giancarlo's drawing of the power meter as a gas pump. Based on his own background knowledge, he drew a red gas pump with the kind of gauges found on gas pumps from the early 1960s, when this story takes place. He put accent lines around his label of "fuel meter" to draw our attention to this gauge. The sign announces "get your gas here." By placing the names of the characters in the gauge, then, Gialcarlo's illustration shows how much each is filled up with energy, or power. As with sketch-to-stretch, the gas pump becomes a metaphor, here for the relative power of characters.

Finally, I include Phillip's power meter (Figure 77c) because it shows the development of one character's use of power across the book. Fifth grader Phillip shows Willy Q's progression in *All of the Above* (Pearsall, 2006) across four levels, distinguishing each level in a few ways. Each level has its own color and box. He also uses emoticons to show their value from mean (Level 1) to loving (Level 4). In each box, Phillip gives an explanation of Willy Q's actions in the plot that shows his progress. Although Willy Q maintained a consistent level of power throughout the book, Phillip shows Willy Q's development toward better uses of power by becoming a better parent to Marcel. Even Phillip's heading expresses meaning. He draws a blaze of red fire in the Q of Willy Q's name because he runs a popular BBQ eatery. On top of LEVELS, Phillip draws the trophy that the math team wins for their tetrahedron project. Above "of Power" he depicts Willie Q's muscular arm with an anchor tattoo that Phillip imagines he got from serving in the Navy.

Narrative Switches

Students created other imaginative responses to critical readings of texts. In *Critical Literacy*, McLaughlin and DeVoogd (2004) discuss exploring *narrative switches:* how might the story change if it took place in a different setting (e.g., *The Wiz* vs. *The Wizard of Oz*), or made a gender switch (e.g., *The Paper Bag Princess*), or was told from an entirely different perspective (e.g., *Wicked* vs. *The Wizard of Oz*), or there was a change in socioeconomic class or of race or nationality (e.g., consider all the variations across the globe of the Cinderella story). These kinds of switches help us to imagine other perspectives, other causes and effects, new sociocultural possibilities. They help us to imagine and perhaps answer "what if" to ultimately develop pluralistic understandings and tolerance for a more humane world.

Figure 78 is one example of a narrative switch. Danya has created a story called "Those Gloves," which she acknowledges on her first page is based on *Those Shoes* (Boelts & Jones, 2007). Danya shows excellent command of narrative writing that appropriates many qualities of *Those Shoes*. In her parallel story, her narrator protagonist is a girl, Isabel, who befriends a girl named Maya. The object of their desire is new gloves, the kind with "silly face characters, like puppets," that all the other girls seem to be able to afford. As in *Those Shoes*, in the end Isabel gives Maya her too-small pair, solidifying their friendship.

In addition to all the benefits of multigenre writing, how does Danya's response express critical literacy? First, she imagines a compelling story about social class from a girl's perspective, and she switches the object of desire from sneakers to gloves. School life in her story now focuses on girls. Second, she raises and contends with new conflicts and resolutions that develop her problem-solving skills and resiliency, such as character relationships between Isabel and her mom. Third, her story pushes Danya to explore important life challenges, such as wants versus needs, being poor, and what it means to be a good friend. Lewison, Flint, and Van Sluys (2002) explain that the first of four dimensions of critical literacy is disrupting the commonplace, which means seeing

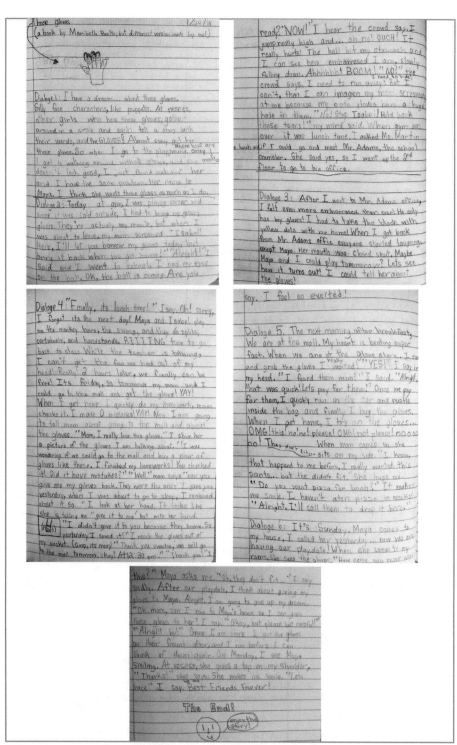

FIGURE 78. Danya's story "Those Gloves" uses the narrative switch strategy.

the everyday through new lenses: "We use language and other sign systems to recognize implicit modes of perception and to consider new frames from which to understand experience" (p. 383). This is what Danya did in her story.

Persuasive Letters

The other three dimensions that Lewison et al. (2002) explain are interrogating multiple viewpoints, focusing on sociopolitical issues, and taking action and promoting social justice. I have shared many examples of the first two dimensions, but some students also used their RRNs to focus on sociopolitical issues. After reading several texts about sharks and making several responses to this information in her RRN, fourth grader Esther wrote a *persuasive letter* to restaurant owners to stop serving shark fin soup (see Figure 79). It's a first draft, and I'm sure you see sev-

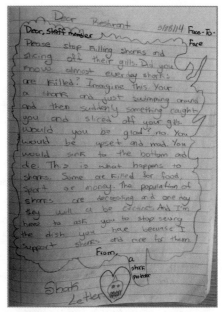

FIGURE 79. Persuasive letter about shark fin soup.

eral ways that Esther can strengthen this letter. But when the class studied persuasive writing a few weeks later, Esther didn't need to begin with gathering ideas; she already had her first draft ready to go. She'd found a sociopolitical issue that mattered to her and she had already accumulated background knowledge about it.

Introspective Journeys

In Chapter 1, I emphasized that one way we monitor students' work in their RRNs toward agency, autonomy, and accountability is through entries that prove they are taking introspective journeys through texts that matter in their lives, as opposed to retrospective accounts (Hancock, 1993). Many of the images I share in this book show this evidence. You see in some of the entries students circling words they are unsure how to spell, erasing, crossing out, inserting words and phrases using carets or in the margins or with arrows, and reworking ideas. It's clear that they are rereading and revising and editing their entries. I also share examples of entries that employ more than one strategy, such as a character list and then a character web of relationships, or a diagram and a chart, or a character list and a power meter. These entries demonstrate how students are thinking about a text in multiple ways. In some entries, students use three or more strategies to think through a text. Eisuke's "Lightning Eleven GO Galaxy" entry (Figure 69) is one example. Figures 80a and b are two more examples.

In Figure 80a, second grader Rachel offers multiple responses to *Oliver Button Is a Sissy* (DePaola, 1979). At the bottom of her response, she indicates her color codes: green for why, purple for labels, and blue for point of view. She also provides two sketch-to-stretch drawings. We learn from her "why" statement that the first one, the eye with a golden star as the iris, represents Oliver Button, who "acts like a star." She places a twinkle in his eye—or suggests that he's seeing stars—that is complementary to the final message in the book: "Oliver Button is a Star!" The second sketch-to-stretch is the happy face inside the pink heart, representing the "girls who stood up for Oliver." Rachel's sketch-to-stretch implies that they are happy and loving. She also includes a representational drawing of a mean boy. The angled eyebrows, beady eyes, and gaping red smiling mouth imply menace. She labels the drawing "Boys that tease Oliver." As indicated on the sticky notes, Rachel chose this as one of her favorite entries: "[I]ts very detailed, and it teaches you to be like Oliver. It explains the moral of the story, and it shows my higher order thinking."

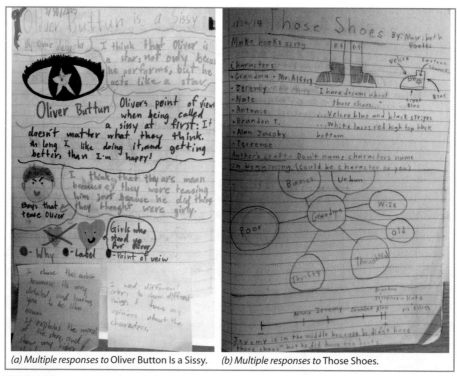

(a) *Multiple responses to* Oliver Button Is a Sissy.　(b) *Multiple responses to* Those Shoes.

FIGURE 80. Examples of multiple responses.

In Figure 80b, fourth grader Yasmin creates multiple responses to think deeply about *Those Shoes* (Boelts & Jones, 2007). She divides her entry into three sections. In the top section, she includes a representational drawing of the fancy shoes on Jeremy's feet, labeling the drawing with a quote from the book and two details about the sneakers. Yasmin also includes a diagram of the Velcro sneakers that Mr. Alfrey provided Jeremy once his old sneakers ripped. On the upper left, Yasmin includes a character list. Beneath this top section, she adds an insight about author's craft that perhaps she could apply to her own story writing. The middle section is a character web for Jeremy's grandma, a pivotal character in the story. Yasmin uses insightful adjectives that describe Grandma. In the bottom section, she draws a power meter to explore the relative power of the characters in the story, explaining why she put Jeremy in the middle. You can imagine the discussions Yasmin now could have with reading partners about this book.

Another proof of students' introspective journeys through texts was the multiple entries they made about one text across pages in their RRNs. Natalie was a third grader in Lori Diamond's class. For *The Battle of the Labyrinth* (Riordan, 2008), she made a coded character list, wrote letters to Annabeth and to Quentus (aka Daedalus), and created an extensive character analysis chart that she added to as she read other books in the series. Similarly, for *Warriors: Fire and Ice* (Hunter & Stevenson, 2015), she described each clan (e.g., Thunderclan, Riverclan, Shadowclan), wrote a letter to Riverclan, and provided an extensive character analysis chart that extended across seven pages. Natalie was one of many students who wrote a variety of thoughtful and elaborate entries for one text that proved their use of the RRN as a tool for introspective journeys through texts.

Summary

In this chapter, I have illustrated how students enacted agency, autonomy, and accountability to their community of learners in their RRNs. They attained Level 3 in our gradual release of responsibility model (see Figure 11). In fact, there was no way for us to keep up. To this day, students constantly surprise us with their innovations. I'm sure that I'll discover new entries by students that will surpass the examples I've shared. I have showcased their innovations for multigenre writing, for recontextualizations of social media and popular culture forms, for reformulations, for connections to popular culture texts, and for critical literacy responses. I've showed how students enacted all four dimensions of literate people (Freebody & Luke, 1990) in their RRN responses: text decoders, text users, meaning makers, and text critics. I've unpacked the deep comprehension and close analytical work, consistent with the demands of state and national standards, in these responses. I've also provided evidence that students were increasingly using their RRNs as tools for introspective journeys through texts. In summary, as we progressed through the school year, students' work became creative, generative, and purposeful. In the next chapter, I share how this journey developed their identities as literate people in the world.

Changing Lives

Literate Identities

What does identity have to do with being a literate person? The operative definition of literacy in this book is tied up in identity. According to Short and Harste (1996), "Literacy is a process of outgrowing our current selves to solve our communicative problems" (p. 32). Literate people read and write in wide, deep, and expansive ways across contexts and media, depending on the sociocultural situations they are in (Jones, Clarke, & Enriquez, 2010). They have a repertoire of literate practices that are purposeful, meaningful, and give them pleasure. Frank Smith (1988) asserts that children want to join the literacy club "because they can see others engaging profitably in literacy activities who are the kind of people the children see themselves as being" (p. 10). Moreover, students will participate if we provide authentic literacy activities that are engaging and accessible. Authentic literacy activities "replicate or reflect reading and writing activities that occur in the lives of people outside of a learning-to-read-and-write context and purpose" (Duke, Purcell-Gates, Hall, & Tower, 2006, p. 346) using real-world texts, like the texts explored in this book. If we provide many opportunities for students' risk-taking, approximations, and affiliation, and guide them to build bridges between school and their everyday literacy practices, they will strive toward proficiency. Their literacy development will become woven into who they are becoming in the world.

In Chapters 3 and 4, I explained the gradual release of responsibility model (see Figure 11) that guided the students of P.S. 144 toward agency, autonomy, and accountability. In this chapter, I explain how these literate behaviors developed from students' identity work. As we saw in several of the examples I shared in Chapters 2 through 5, students had several opportunities to choose and share favorite entries using sticky notes. We also had students write reflections twice each year in their RRNs about what they were learning from this work. Toward the end of each school year, I held whole-class discussions about their notebook work. I also interviewed six students—one second grader, one third grader, three fourth graders, and one fifth grader—audio recording all discussions and interviews. The six students lent me their notebooks so that, as they walked me through their favorite notebook entries, I could follow along at home. I transcribed all audio recordings and read through all students' notebook reflections, and then used grounded theory (Charmaz, 2000) to identify categories of what accounted for their development of agency, autonomy, and accountability. Five dominant categories emerged: *creativity, deep comprehension, keeping track of their reading, reading/writing connections,* and *social interactions.* Students' comments in each of these categories expressed their growing *identities* as literate people. In the next section, I explain what students expressed in each category, providing examples in their own words. (Please note that, in all instances, I transcribed students' written reflections using their own spelling and punctuation.) I then share their teachers' experiences with implementing this work. I conclude the chapter with some final thoughts about this book and examples of students' entries from Lesley Doff's fifth-grade class.

What Students Learned

Creativity

One way students expressed learning from their RRN work was through opportunities for *creative responses.* A primary expression of creativity was responding to important texts in their lives, such as keeping ongoing lists (see Figures 20 and 21), or the examples I discussed in Figures 69 through 73. Figure 81a shows one favorite entry that fourth grader Dyandra shared with me. This entry consists of questions to Jeremy Strong, the author of *Romans on the Rampage!* (Strong & Clifford, 2015), that Dyandra wrote in Indonesian. Then, on the back of the page, she wrote the English translation (Figure 81b). Dyandra explained: "Because my mom said to me, when I first came here to the United States, 'Whatever you do, don't forget your Indonesian language.' So, she inspired me to write a response with Indonesian language." She explained how she had the freedom to explore this kind of response in her RRN, and this helped make sure that "I'll always remember my Indonesian language."

Many students shared that they could represent their feelings and emotions for texts they read, emphasizing the expressiveness they found possible in their notebooks. Fifth grader Ella wrote in her reflection:

> . . .[I]t was the one notebook that allowed me to express my feelings and emotions. It also helped me with keeping my thoughts, questions, and wonders. . . .
> With my notebook, I've also been allowed to get down my creative ideas. The

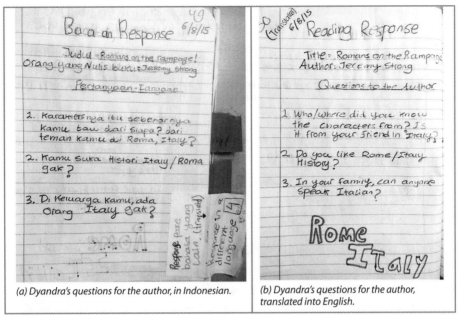

(a) Dyandra's questions for the author, in Indonesian.

(b) Dyandra's questions for the author, translated into English.

FIGURE 81. Dyandra's creative responses.

reader response notebook is more like a partner that understands everything that you're trying to say and helps you organize your own thoughts and emotions and feelings.

Students were motivated to find creative ways to express these affective responses to texts. Phillip, another fifth grader, provided an example in his reflection:

> I think the Reading Response Notebook is a great opertunity to show our feelings and creativity.... I don't think of our writing as a big boring essay anymore, I think of writing as a colorful drawing that will make my Reading Response Notebook come alive. I think the Reading Response Notebook really shows who we are and how creative we are.

In Chapter 5, I shared many examples of these strong emotional responses and unpacked what these responses revealed about readers' emotional and intellectual participation in each literary text as a whole. These responses and students' reflections about these responses express Louise Rosenblatt's (1938/1995) conception of reading as an active and creative transaction between the reader and the text. Rosenblatt emphasizes reading literature as exploration. We don't simply read for new content knowledge; rather, we live *through* the reading experience. Rosenblatt calls this "evoking the world of the text":

The greater the reader's ability to respond to the stimulus of the word and the greater his capacity to savor all that words can signify of rhythm, sound, and image, the more fully will he be emotionally and intellectually able to participate in the literary work as a whole. In return, literature will help the reader sharpen further his alertness to the sensuous quality of experience. (p. 48)

As students themselves expressed, these transactions with texts are pleasurable. Fourth grader Jonathan, for example, loved that "you can use your imagination to shape the story in your own way."

Some students described "thinking outside the box" for their creative responses. They were emphatic that the creative possibilities deepened their reading comprehension. Fifth grader Evan stated:

The reader response notebook helped me as a reader by making me more creative while responded to a book. This is relevant because getting more creative helps me think more....It also gets me wondering, how do the characters change, what will happen next, what will this character do, and other advanced questions.

Students experienced firsthand what Louise Rosenblatt (1938/1995) asserts:

The young reader's personal involvement in a work will generate greater sensitivity to its imagery, style, and structure; this in turn will enhance his understanding of its human implications. A reciprocal process emerges, in which growth in human understanding and literary sophistication sustain and nourish each other. Both kinds of growth are essential if the student is to develop the insight and the skill needed for participation in increasingly complex and significant literary works. (p. 52)

Deep Comprehension

Students also expressed how valuable the RRN was as a tool to develop *deep comprehension* of texts, of having many strategies for thinking deeply, either as an introspective journey for one text, or using or inventing just the right strategy to explore their ideas for particular texts. Fourth grader Emil commented:

We always learned new strategies that are on our strategies list. And we always read a book and then did one of those new strategies that we learned. These strategies help us because now, each time we read a book, we can always figure out the morals or what the author is thinking about in this book. These strategies that we learned definitely helped us with our reading level.

Students expressed much more agency as a result of learning to apply strategies. Fifth grader Phillip reflected: "I can now think of a creative 'entry' in my mind while I am reading a book and think more about that book." In our whole-class discussion in Lesley Doff's fifth-grade class, Sean commented:

> The reading response notebook's encouraging me a lot more to actually respond to a text, because I realize there're so many different ways to respond to it. In the old reading response notebook, there were really only around five ways to do it, and it had to be correct, and the teacher had to like it, or else you got a bad grade on it. But this is much more creative, so now I actually like responding to my reading.

Hannah then responded that in the old notebook, they wrote more literal responses, only "what the actual words were." "But now we dig deeper and actually read between the lines, and have multiple answers." Karas, another fourth grader, commented:

> [W]hen I do readers' response, I actually realize that I think about all the connections and everything, and I realize that the author maybe meant for us to do that. It's really cool to realize that the author actually put a lot of work into it, and my responses help me discover that.

I suspect that Sofie spoke for most students: "The books have become more interesting."

One dimension of deep comprehension that students mentioned often was their newfound ability to perceive multiple perspectives as a result of applying so many reader response strategies. In our whole-class discussion in Deb Kessler's fourth grade, Evelyn said, "I understand the characters more and their perspectives. I could use different ways to write, draw, or color about my book that I'm reading." Samantha then shared her response. When Chris asked what she meant by "Another way my readers notebook helped me see books in different angles and different words," Samantha responded, "Because sometimes books don't always show, they only show one perspective or way. But there's many more perspectives to see."

CHRIS: Uh, so you're like changing the book around to see **differently**?
SAMANTHA: **Yeah**.

The boldfaced dialogue indicates overlapping speech, which shows how emphatically Samantha was able to affirm what Chris asked. She now knows that you can challenge authors, even change their stories, by presenting the story from other perspectives. Fifth grader Samantha wrote, "My reading response notebook has encouraged me to think about what I read in multiple ways." In other words, her creative use of strategies allowed her to see much more complexity in all the texts she read.

Keeping Track of Their Reading

Students also expressed the value of the RRN as *a tool to keep track of and organize their thinking*. In my interview with fourth grader Sophia, she stated:

> I could write down what I've learned from reading books. . . . It helps me keep track of everything I've ever read. . . . I could always look back to keep learning from what I've already read and always remember it. . . . I could always add more to what I've already learned.

Other students, such as third grader Victor, noted that the notebook helped to "organize" their thinking. Victor explained that he paid closer attention to "facts in books that I might otherwise have disregarded. It made me pay attention to details, and it made me reflect on the characters more." He wrote that jotting down notes "was important for reading a book that you can not finish in one sitting or even a few days." In addition, the RRN helped him track his own progress as a reader. Jeremiah, also in Lori Diamond's third-grade class, concurred. In his reflection, he wrote:

> Keeping my reading response notebook helped me as a reader because this notebook has all my thoughts about all the books I read. I could read all my responses over and over again. So I might be interested in reading the books again that I wrote about.

Many students expressed how, without their deliberate RRN work, they would have read a book and moved on to another one without ever pausing to reflect on and learn from each book. Some students, such as Caitlin, considered this from a remarkably practical angle: "But in 4th grade every idea about a book that we have read is joted down so that when we are older we can look back and remeber ower ideas." As with learning strategies, students appreciated the agency of keeping a reader response notebook. Fourth grader Amanda wrote that keeping this notebook "made me more responesable and I started doing more thing's on my own."

Reading-Writing Connections

Several students commented on *reading-writing connections,* such as the volume of their writing and language use. Third grader Ben wrote:

> This reading response notebook helped me as a writer by making me write lots of details and making me write more than I used to. It showed me to just write down your idea's and everything in the book will come out.

Victor wrote:

> My RRN helped me use better vocabulary. Some of the responses asked us to use more complex adjectives and adverbs. In addition, in writing the reading re-sponses, I learned to make more complex sentences. In this way, I learned how to connect ideas and use punctuation correctly.

Students commented on learning to write more neatly as a result of account-ability: yes, because the teacher gave them a maintenance score on the grading criteria, but even more because they sometimes "passed the notebook" in share sessions when their classmates commented on their work. They also learned what kind of writing they liked. Third grader Sylvan wrote, "I learned that I like writing character lists and letters to the character." Students also appreciated the opportunities to use many kinds of writing tools in addition to plain pencils, such as markers, colored pencils, crayons, and pens.

Social Interactions

Students also expressed the value of the *social interactions* of their RRN work. Dyandra shared how she loved her dialogic entries in which characters spoke back and forth to each other. These entries "were inspired by the fifth grade stu-dents" who visited her class one morning to share notebook entries. In our class discussion in Deb Kessler's class, Jason shared:

> Also, when we share each others, and say we're in the same group, and we read the same book, but had different ideas, you could follow along with one of the student's ideas, or be inspired by that way of thinking about the book.

One of Dyandra's favorite entries was a creative display of a power meter for *Dork Diaries: Tales from a Not-So-Fabulous Life* (Russell, 2010; Figure 82). She

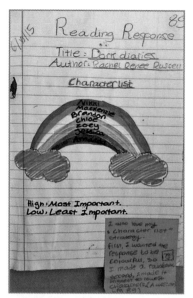

FIGURE 82. Dyandra's character list for a Dork Diaries book.

shared that a new girl in class was "actually inspired by me to make a character list as a rainbow also, but organized her colors differently."

Students noted that RRNs helped them to prepare for reading partners and small-group discussions. Fourth grader Caitlin explained that discussions were difficult for her:

> But in my reading response notebook, I can jot down ideas, my thinking, instead of having to think of words on the spot, so it makes it easier for me, and then I can just show my partner the work that I did, and it [her response] explained it [her thoughts] much better than if I say it in words.

In her reflection entry, she elaborated:

> For example I was reading *Whatever Ever After Cold as Ice* [Mlynowski, 2014]. It was hard to explain what was happening but when I should my friend my Reading Response she understood it and I understood it so much better than trying to explain it just with words.

Sophia, a fifth grader, wrote, "Now when I read I pay more attention to detail. This helps me talk about the book more and learn to conversationanize with my fellow classmates."

Identity

Many of the student quotes I have shared contained *identity* statements. Recall, for example, what Dyandra said about her Indonesian language, or all of the students' self-awareness of their own reading and writing development. Fifth grader Alyssa stated, "The RRN made me another person in a way. Now, when I read, I think more about the characters and whats going to happen and all the things we do in the RRN." Sean, a third grader, wrote how the use of this RRN influenced his identity:

> Now I feall that I have grown not just as a reader but as a writer. I feal like this notebook helped me learn that I am smarter than I think. I have descoverd a likeing for books and especaly comics and long chapter books. When I uset to look at books it just looks like a book but now I see how inspiring the true story is. it is so amazing how geting your ideas out on papper can make you so intrested in

books and what the authers rote. It makes you just want to sit down and write somthing just like it.

Figure 83 is an entry from fifth grader Elizabeth. She designed her entry to look like an open double-page spread of her notebook. The right-hand page is a sketch-to-stretch. People who *can* change the world fill the entire area of the bottom rectangle in yellow highlighter. People who *actually* change the world are represented by tiny isolated yellow highlighter circles with blue outlines in the upper rectangle. Her sketch-to-stretch implies that while all people have the capacity to change the world, only an isolated few actually do. On the left-hand page, Elizabeth emphasized: "All throughout my notebook my entries represent being a good person. If I try to put those lessons into every day life, I and those around me will become better people." Elizabeth's identity statement expresses her desire to achieve the highest dimension of critical literacy in the framework by Lewison et al. (2002): taking action and promoting social justice.

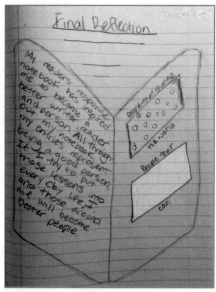

FIGURE 83. Elizabeth's final reflection.

Teachers' Experiences with RRNs

I checked in with teachers in several ways about using RRNs. For most school visits, teachers and I co-taught lessons to their students for new RRN strategies. We then met during lunch to discuss how their students did with the new strategy and next steps. We also focused on specific topics we were investigating, such as trying out strategies from one of the professional books, or how we might assess students' notebook work, or how we might support students' autonomy with the strategies we taught. I kept notes and reflections in a notebook, and after each visit, I wrote a group email that summarized our work for the day, prepared everyone for my next visit, and included attachments of forms, worksheets, and checklists that we used. Our problem solving led to solutions such as the RRN Strategy Checklist we developed (see Figure 39 and Appendix A). We always ended each meeting with plans for my next visit. To further support this work, principal Reva Gluck-Schneider supported the teachers' work as a study group throughout the entire school year. They met every Wednesday afternoon, when other teacher study groups met. In our interviews, the teachers told me that this is when they especially shared "how's it going" in their classrooms, shared ideas and resources, reviewed our group blog, and posted to their own blogs.

In the first year of this project, the teachers each kept a blog about their class's use of RRNs, and all of these were hosted on a central blog that I maintained (rrn2013.blogspot.com). On this central blog, I had the following links: Home, Links, and Resources. The homepage included posts that, like my emails, summarized our discussions after each of my visits. On the Links page, I provided links to useful resources that we relied on for our ongoing work. Similarly, on the Resources page, I provided materials for the RRN strategies we taught our students. The blog became another resource for our ongoing communication. We also held end-of-the-year reflection sessions to discuss how the RRN work had gone. These sessions were audio recorded, and I later transcribed and analyzed them for the teachers' insights. In this section, I synthesize our insights from all of these sources, using, as much as possible, the teachers' own words. My purpose is to share our collective wisdom to support your own journey of implementing these new ways of using the RRN with students.

The teachers placed enormous value on students' agency, autonomy, and accountability. These behaviors demanded that students mature over time as readers and writers. Lori Diamond commented:

> I think we all agree that it took us a really long time for our kids to own it, to have the confidence for them to know what to do without us telling them what to do, and then for them to take it seriously and try their hardest. And that takes time and routine.

Lauren Heinz elaborated:

> It took us all year, but they're finally doing their own stuff on their own, coming up with new strategies, not just the ones we give them. You know, they're really taking their ownership to it now. Whereas in the beginning, we gave them one strategy, that's the only strategy they did. And they only did it when we told them to do it. Now I feel that they're a lot more independent. They feel a lot more free about coming up with their own strategies, or using the strategies we taught them, but maybe in a little bit different way to fit the need of their books and their ideas.

The teachers noted that what helped encourage students' accountability were the grading criteria (see Chapter 3). However, they were useful only if the teachers applied them consistently. The teachers discussed marking students' notebooks table by table, one table each day, every two weeks. Equally important for student accountability was a strong sense of audience. Lori noted, "They're writing for an audience: whether it's me or their peers," which gave them pleasure. As a result, the students had "pride in their work. Pride in their penmanship, pride in their spelling, pride in their thoughts."

The teachers emphasized that the RRN work made their students better readers, in accordance with state and national standards. Lesley Doff explained:

> I thought it was really interesting for the kids to be able to look at all different kinds of texts in many different ways, and then have to prove what they were saying and what they were thinking, using more text evidence. So, no matter what they were doing, they had to dive back into the text to prove their point. We were always doing close reading. We were always deep reading, and doing our regular ELA work, and I think this made it easier for them.

Lauren Heinz found the RRN equally valuable for nonfiction reading.

> You know, we did a lot of nonfiction this year. Having their reader response notebooks out there for non-fiction, I think, made them slow down, because they tend to read non-fiction just as fast as they read fiction, and they don't hold onto it. And it made them slow it down, take a close look at what they were reading, and try to think of it in a different way. And a lot of our coming up to them was like, "Look what I found, I'm gonna make a graph out of this." "Can I put this in a diagram? Can I make a diagram of this?" And I'm just like, "Go ahead." You know. "You do what you want to do." And they get excited when they find an idea that they want to use.

The RRN provided a tool for developing these habits of mind. Lesley said, "It became the habit that that's how we looked at every single text, as opposed to, 'Well, this is just what it says, so that's what I'm gonna say.'"

The teachers had to figure out a balance for reader response work. Lori, always a pragmatist, commented:

> It's impractical to say they're going to do this five days a week. They're going to do it, they'll read in the class five days a week, and they're going to write reflectively five days a week, in their notebook. It's not going to happen.

All the teachers found a balance between writing two to three responses each week between schoolwork and homework, and they sent the RRNs for homework only after students were very familiar with the routines and expectations. Lauren Heinz presented her practical solution:

Sometimes if we wanted to write in the classroom, that would count as one of the three entries. You know. If we sat and did an entry together in the classroom, it's not two to three on top of what we did in class with me. That counts as one. So, they would say, "Oh, yeah, we're doing one now, so I don't have to do one tonight." You know. So, it was two to three entries a week, inside of class and out, you know, mixed together, and it wasn't a given day's assignment for homework, as long as they met or exceeded their quota for the week.

The teachers also discussed the strength of the collaborative work of our professional development. As I stated previously, they learned extensively from one another. But they also noted relying on my expertise. Deb Kessler commented:

The problem is, it's not as if we can't do these things, or more of them, but I think there's a combination of collaboration that makes this whole notebook come alive, which I just think that's part of it. If we took you out of the equation, you know, if there was another you, then possibly. But then it would have to be something a little bit more.... It's almost like, you know when you bring an author in? You're like that famous person. So, it brought the whole level up.

And while I can't be physically present in *your* journey toward using the RRN in the ways illustrated in this book, you now have this book to serve as your source of expertise.

Ultimately, the teachers emphasized, the RRN brought their students pleasure. They expressed how, in all their years of using RRNs, as Lauren stated: "My students enjoyed the readers notebook the most I've ever seen." She explained that in previous years,

my kids weren't really coming up with strong ideas; they were just reading. And then, when they told you about what they were writing, it was the basic plot. You know, mechanical, this is what my book's about. And now I feel, more so even than the improvement in their writing, their ideas and the way they are thinking about the books has improved dramatically.

Lesley expressed similar sentiments:

It was really nice to see my kids excited about writing about their reading. Because in the past, it's always been "Write a three-sentence summary, show me your connection" or something that puts you to sleep that they didn't want to write and I didn't want to read. Now, I want to look at all their notebooks, and I want to read all their notebooks, and I want to talk about it. It's really interesting.

They have great things to say, and it [their notebook responses] has opened so much, and they are able to be free about what they have to say, their opinions, their thoughts, and the choice of entries are so wide, and it is great to see them so excited about it.

Where We Go from Here

The teachers and I took on the challenges of using the RRN in the ways I've described because we are committed to teaching and learning as an ongoing process, consistent with what Short and Harste (1996) describe as the Authoring Cycle. As the Authoring Cycle suggests, we began by **building from the known**. We brought our collective knowledge of reader response notebooks. As both teachers and students expressed, they had all experienced past frustrations with the usual responses. Building on reader response ideas from Albers (2007), Bomer (2011), Buckner (2009), Calkins (2001), Fountas and Pinnell (2001), Rief (2007), Romano (2013), Short and Harste (1996), and others, and especially my own collective experiences as a classroom teacher and teacher educator, I was able to infuse new life into the same-old tired work they had been doing. This collective knowledge led to the first phase of our authoring cycle: **taking the time to formulate inquiry questions.** We wondered what kinds of responses might be possible if we expanded what counts as a text and opened up responses to design work. We wondered how we might develop students' capacities for agency, autonomy, and accountability for reader response. We wondered how these ways of thinking in a dialogic community might both support our need to address mandates and standards AND facilitate students' development as literate people.

In the introduction, I brought up some other inquiry questions that are worth restating here: (a) What range of reader responses might elementary and middle school students express if we made available to them a variety of resources? (b) How might we design instruction so that students develop autonomy that matches their reading purposes in their use of reader response notebooks? (c) What does this variety of response show about students' reading comprehension? (d) How does opening up what counts as text influence their literate identities and their development as readers? (e) How might we use their notebooks as tools to develop a literate community of practice? (f) How does this notebook work support students' collaborative discussions and their written responses (e.g., essays), aligned with state and national standards? (g) How might we guide students toward self-assessment of their notebook work? (h) In what ways do these notebooks, used in the ways we continue to develop, become tools for students living literate lives? These are the inquiry questions I address in this book. My work with the teachers at P.S. 144 demonstrates that by extending and broadening what counts as text and the possibilities of designing on the page, by greenlighting a wide variety of responses, and by valuing these practices as important literate behaviors, we are expanding what it means to be readers and writers in school settings (Bloome, 1985) and who can join the literacy club (Smith, 1988).

The second phase in our authoring cycle was **gaining new perspectives**. Earlier I described the ways that the teachers and I continually gained new perspectives through co-teaching lessons, lunchtime debriefing meetings, the teachers' weekly study group, our study group blogs, summary emails, sharing resources, and reflection sessions. Phase 3 was **attending to difference,** exemplified in Chapter 3 when I discussed the ongoing anchor chart of strategies we taught students, and in Chapter 4 when I described all the ways that we learned from students, revised our thinking, created checklists and grading criteria, and thought through our plans for implementation. Phase 4 was **sharing what was learned**. In Chapter 4, I also discussed sharing sessions and other opportunities for reflection we conducted with students. These sessions created communities of practice that supported students' agency, autonomy, and accountability. Students felt safe to build bridges to their own sociocultural literacy practices, as illustrated in Chapter 5 and Dyandra's Indonesian language examples (see Figure 81).

Our work has certainly led us to Phase 5: **planning new inquiries**. Teachers described how long it took them to teach a range of strategies that the students could eventually use flexibly with agency, autonomy, and accountability. None of us has had the opportunity to work with a group of students who have done this RRN work for two or more years in succession. Currently, we can only imagine how much easier it would be to unfold this work, and how much further students would take it, if these practices were consistent across all classes in a grade and in all grades 2 through 8 in a school district.

Limitations

As I stated in the introduction, while I have been pursuing this inquiry my entire teaching career and bring all of those years of experience to the writing of this book, the majority of the examples come from the particular context of one school. As all worthy inquiry projects should do, we invite you to continue this line of inquiry in your own settings, reporting on your own particular contexts with diverse student populations. I especially worry about students who, for various reasons, have acquired school-based labels of "struggling reader" or "at-risk" because of reading difficulties, with debilitating consequences. Might this expansive and creative approach to reader response change who these readers can be? As I describe in Chapter 2, a particular benefit of this RRN work is that it allows students to build from the known. Consequently, we teachers are able to discover who they are, what they do well, what literacy practices matter to them, and, ultimately, how they can teach us to teach them better. Therefore, we believe that this RRN work enables us to apply "turn-around pedagogies" (Jones et al., 2010) that might guide these students toward productive reading identities.

The teachers of P.S. 144 and I invite you to pursue these or other inquiry plans as well. We invite you to share your own discoveries as you pursue your own authoring cycle for new applications of this RRN work. Recall the RRN blog that we kept for this project (rrn2013.blogspot.com). We have now created a new blog, readerresponsenotebook.blogspot.com, also available via the QR code below on your mobile device. We invite you to contribute your comments as you embark on your own RRN inquiry projects with your students. We also invite you to use #readerresponsenotebook on Twitter, which will feed on my website (www.tedsclassroom.com). Let's create our own virtual learning community by sharing our challenges, questions, and successes.

Conclusion

One day, in a playful mood, Lesley Doff invited her students to write an RRN response to you, the reader of this book. This book had not yet been written, so students had to imagine what they might say, how they might say it, and who this audience might be. Basically, they were perfectly set up for multigenre writing (Romano, 2013), and like many of their multigenre explorations, we received a wide range of wonderful responses. I close the book with four that perhaps you can share with colleagues to entice them to pursue this work. In Figures 84a and b, Bryan and Sandy wrote their invitations as a blurb for the back of the book. In Figure 85, David wrote his invitation as a petition, advocating for the use of this notebook "in every school." Obviously, as the author of this book, I certainly promote David's advocacy. Finally, in Figure 86, Emma wrote her invitation as a comic strip in which the narrator promotes this book. As always, when we provided opportunities to "play around," we were delighted in students' creativity, seriousness of purpose, and insightfulness. We were so proud of their expressions of agency, autonomy, and accountability, and the strength of their burgeoning literate identities.

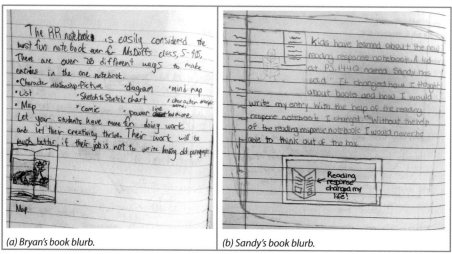

(a) Bryan's book blurb.   (b) Sandy's book blurb.

FIGURE 84. Examples of book blurbs.

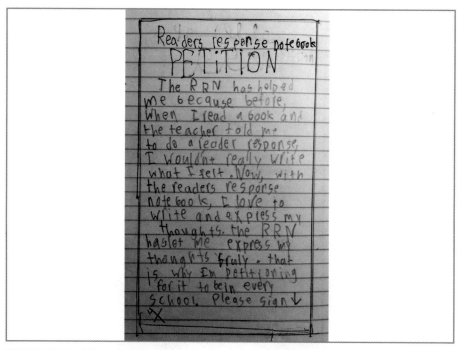

FIGURE 85. David's petition.

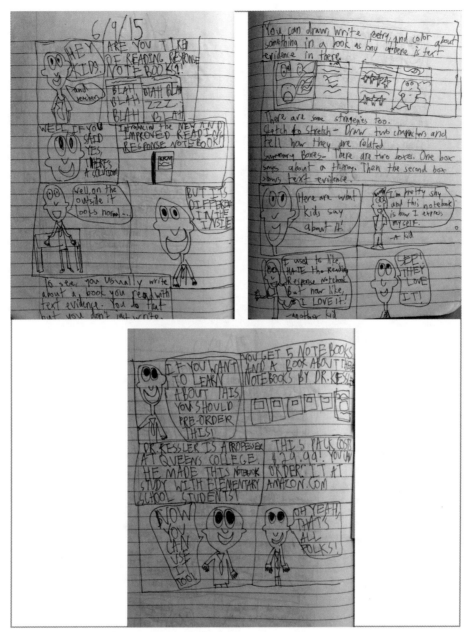

FIGURE 86. Emma's three-page comic.

Appendix A

RRN Strategy Checklist

Readers Notebook Strategies

NAME:

	Date	Date	Date	Date
Sketch-to-Stretch				
Summary Boxes				
Representational Drawing				
Character List				
Character Web of Relationships				
The Subtext Strategy				
Writing the Blurb				
Letter to the character, to the author, or between characters				
Reformulations—Chart, Graph, Diagram				
Critical Literacy: Writing from the perspective of a character who has a limited voice				
Critical Literacy: Asking questions of characters				
Critical Literacy: Writing a letter from one character to another.				
Critical Literacy: Writing "the untold story": what is NOT said in the text that should be said				
Found Poetry				
Leaning In				
Digging In				
Lifting a Line				
Other:				
Other:				
Other:				
Ongoing lists:				

Appendix B

RRN Grading Criteria

Name: _____   Date: _____

Notebook Checklist

	1	2	3	4	5
Volume					
Variety					
Thoughtfulness					
Maintenance					

Additional Comments:

Reader's Response

1. Do you agree with my evaluation? Why or why not?

2. How can I (the teacher) help?

3. What will *you* (the student) do?

* See the back of this checklist for **Expectations**.

Notebook Expectations

Volume: You write *two* or *three* entries per week. Some entries have lots of writing and take up a page or longer. Some entries use other modes or forms of expression. You also keep three or more ongoing lists in the back of your notebook.

Variety: You write *some* expository entries. These entries may use sentence starters. These entries may summarize the plot or explain information you learned. Other entries use other modes of expression: responses to quotes; ways you are planning to use information in a text; drawings; maps; timelines; graphic organizers; etc. You are also exploring a variety of texts: nonfiction, fiction, poetry, but also articles, photos, artwork, performances, TV shows, video games, etc.

Thoughtfulness: I hear *your* voice when I read your notebook. Your entries do not feel like you wrote them just "to get them over with." Many entries feel like you were thinking your way through a text, like you realize something now that you never realized before. You ask yourself questions that you might or might not yet have the answers for. You make a few entries about one text as you work your way through it. You explore various ways to make meaning from a text.

Maintenance: You take good care of your notebook by:
- a. putting the date and maybe a page number for each new entry
- b. using every page and not skipping pages
- c. working *neatly* enough to be able to re-read entries easily
- d. using spacing that makes it easy to *edit, revise,* or *nurture* your entries
- e. showing evidence of editing: punctuation and spelling

Appendix C

RRN Strategies Anchor Chart

RRN STRATEGY CHART			
STRATEGY	**WHAT**	**WHY**	**EXAMPLE**
Sketch-to-Stretch	Make a sketch using colors, lines, shapes, symbols. Write a title and a caption that explains your sketch.	• To explore character relationships or qualities of a character • To explore conflicts in a story • To explore how setting influences characters	
Representational Drawing	Make a sketch or drawing using colors, as if you were hired as the illustrator of the text. Rely on details in the text. Write a title and a caption that explains your drawing.	• To envision the setting • To envision an important object or character or event that is carefully described in the text	
Parking Lot	Jot down notes and impressions as you read or listen or view the text. You might record buzzwords, key phrases, predictions, wonderings, key plot developments, new information, a quote. Use bullets or numbered statements. Write shorthand.	• To record your impressions of the text in the process of reading it • To review your impressions to gain new insights and develop theories about the text	
Summary Boxes	After each section or chapter of a text, give a summary in one or two of the boxes in the chart.	• To remember what you've read so far, especially if it takes a few days to finish the text	

Essence Chart	After each section or chapter of a text, write what you think is the most important, interesting, or essential part.	• To pay attention to new or surprising or compelling parts of a story, biography, or informational text	
List of Characters	Keep an ongoing list of characters. You might use symbols to indicate central or secondary characters, animals, Muggles, children, or evil characters, etc.	• To sort out and keep track of characters in a story, especially when there are lots of them (e.g., the Harry Potter books or a favorite TV series)	
Character Web of Relationships	Create a web of characters' names. Use colors, lines, shapes, spacing, special fonts, and other symbols to show the connections between characters. Be sure to include a key or legend that explains your use of colors, lines, and other symbols.	• To show the relationships among characters	
Found Poetry	Create a poem using key phrases from a text and poetry elements, such as repetition, line breaks, stanzas, a refrain, a title. While you can put phrases in any sequence, you are not allowed to alter the words.	• To develop an aesthetic appreciation for the craft of writing in the text • To use poetic elements to express the essence of a text	

Reformulations	Use other forms or genres to reformulate the content of a text. For example, you might use a flow map to show a process, a chart to show different categories of animals, a diagram to show a living thing, a graph to show a growth cycle, a poem to appreciate beautiful language.	• To think more about information in a text • To represent information in a new way • To use creativity to imagine new possibilities for a text	
Multigenre Writing[a]	Similar to reformulations. Write a section of the text or the ending of the text or the entire text in another form or genre, such as a song, a script, a poem, a flyer, an advertisement, etc.	• To imagine new forms and genres of writing for the topic, issue, or plot of the text • To gain new insights about the topic, issue, or plot of the text by imagining other forms and genres of writing • To appreciate the craft and genre of writing of the original text	
A Letter to a Character or the Author or Illustrator	The letter may be from another character or from you as the reader. For example: "If Wilbur could write a letter to Charlotte at the end of the book, what would he write?"	• To respond directly to the actions, behaviors, or state of mind of a central character • To enable characters to express their thoughts and feelings directly to one another • To express your thoughts and feelings about key characters, events, issues, or depictions directly to the author or illustrator	
Venn Diagram or H-Chart or Modified T-Chart	These charts are great for compare-and-contrast work. The middle space in the H-chart or the bottom section of a T-chart is for attributes that are the same.	• To compare and contrast topics, issues, categories, characters, texts, or different forms of the same story (e.g., the book vs. the movie)	

T-Chart	Set up the chart with two columns. Give each column a heading. Fill in the chart as you read to gather evidence or to think more deeply about information or events in the text.	• To gather evidence about a character, character relation-ships, events, or topic that is the focus of the text • To reflect on key moments, events, or issues in the text	
Timeline	The timeline might be horizontal or vertical. Plot points are time intervals or dates. Each plot point marks a key event.	• To show key events in a life cycle or for historical events	
Flow Map	Key moments are shown in boxes with directional arrows showing the next step in the process.	• To show a process or a sequence of events, leading to a final prod-uct or end result	
Responding Mathematically	Use concepts in math, such as number equa-tions, fractions, line or bar graphs, or pie charts, to think about events, information, character relationships, or plot.	• To express your thinking in a different symbol system (rather than words)	
Draw a Map	Make a map of the set-ting.	• To help envision key events as they occur in the text	

Close Reading Strategies:[b] • Leaning In (an envisioning strategy)	a. Box a few sentences that you want to envision. b. Copy it on a new page in your notebook (include page numbers). c. In your notebook, fill in details of that scene or event.	• To fill in details that you envision but the author (or illustrator) did not provide	
• Digging Deeper (an inferring strategy)	a. Box or underline a line or a few sentences. b. Copy it on a new page in your notebook (include page numbers). c. In your notebook, explain what these lines mean. For example, in *The Man Who Walked between the Towers*: "As long as he stayed on the wire, he was free." What might this mean?	• To think more deeply about key lines in a text	
• Lifting a Line (an interpreting strategy)	a. In your notebook, copy an inspiring, compelling, or important line or few sentences (include page numbers). b. Write what you find inspiring, compelling, or important about this quote.	• To respond to an inspiring, compelling, or important statement by the author or a particular character	
Critical Literacy Strategies:[c] • Mind/Alternative Mind (a perspective strategy)	Draw the profiles of two key characters from the text who are in some kind of relationship. Inside the head of each profile or using thought bubbles, show the thinking from each character's perspective.	• To imagine the voices of different characters about particular events or issues	

• The Missing Voice	Write in the voice of a marginal character who has limited voice in the text or who is missing from the text but should be heard.	• To give voice to a person who should be made more prominent or who would provide an intriguing challenge to what is presented in the text	
• Writing "the Untold Story"	What is NOT said in the text that should be said; what information is missing?	• To fill in information that should be included • To provide perspectives that may be missing from the text • To give voice to people, places, or issues that were left out	
• Power Meter	Consider who has power in a story, or how one person's power shifts in the course of the plot. You might depict this in writing, as a line graph, or any other visual display.	• To consider power differentials among characters • To consider characters in the larger context of the forces acting upon them in the world of the story • To consider how characters use power for their own purposes, or to do good or to do harm to others	
End-of-Reading Strategies: • What Have I Learned	Take stock of what you learned: life lessons; about a social issue; about the topic. This might be a bulleted list, or written as paragraphs, or depicted visually.	• To process and synthesize important information that you might want to remember	

• Write the Blurb	Write what might be on the back cover of the book for a sequel.	• To imagine the focus or plot premise of the sequel	
• An Alternative Ending	Not happy with the ending? How might you write a more satisfying ending?	• To imagine an alternative way the story or events might go	
• Imagine the Characters in the Future	What might become of a character or key characters in the future? Write their bios.	• To imagine how characters continue to develop in the future world beyond the book	

a. From *Fearless Writing* by Tom Romano
b. From *Notebook Connections* by Aimee Buckner
c. From *Critical Literacy* by McLaughlin and DeVoogd

References

Albers, P. (2007). *Finding the artist within: Creating and reading visual texts in the English language arts classroom.* Newark, DE: International Reading Association.

Anderson, C. (2000). *How's it going? A practical guide to conferring with student writers.* Portsmouth, NH: Heinemann.

Bakhtin, M. M. (1986). *Speech genres and other late essays* (V. W. McGee, Trans). Austin: University of Texas Press.

Beers, K. (2003). *When kids can't read, what teachers can do: A guide for teachers 6–12.* Portsmouth, NH: Heinemann.

Bloome, D. (1985). Reading as a social process. *Language Arts, 62*(2), 134–42.

Bomer, R. (2011). *Building adolescent literacy in today's English classrooms.* Portsmouth, NH: Heinemann.

Buckner, A. (2009). *Notebook connections: Strategies for the reader's notebook.* Portland, ME: Stenhouse.

Calkins, L. M. (2001). *The art of teaching reading.* New York: Longman.

Charmaz, K. (2000). Grounded theory: Objectivist and constructivist methods. In N. K. Denzin & Y. S. Lincoln (Eds.), *Handbook of qualitative research* (2nd ed., pp. 509–36). Thousand Oaks, CA: SAGE.

Cudd, E. T., & Roberts, L. (1989). Using writing to enhance content area learning in the primary grades. *The Reading Teacher, 42*(6), 392–404.

Dolby, N. (2003). Popular culture and democratic practice. *Harvard Educational Review, 73*(3), 258–84.

Dorn, L. J., & Soffos, C. (2005). *Teaching for deep comprehension: A reading workshop approach.* Portland, ME: Stenhouse.

Duke, N. K., & Pearson, P. D. (2002). Effective practices for developing reading comprehension. In A. E. Farstrup & S. J. Samuels (Eds.), *What research has to say about reading instruction* (3rd ed., pp. 205–42). Newark, DE: International Reading Association.

Duke, N. K., Purcell-Gates, V., Hall, L. A., & Tower, C. (2006). Authentic literacy activities for developing comprehension and writing. *The Reading Teacher, 60*(4), 344–55.

Dyson, A. H. (2003a). *The brothers and sisters learn to write: Popular literacies in childhood and school cultures.* New York: Teachers College Press.

Dyson, A. H. (2003b). "Welcome to the Jam": Popular culture, school literacy, and the making of childhoods. *Harvard Educational Review, 73*(3), 328–61.

Eisner, E. W. (1998). *The enlightened eye: Qualitative inquiry and the enhancement of educational practice.* Upper Saddle River, NJ: Merrill/Prentice Hall.

Feathers, K. (1993). Text reformulation or story recycling. *Infotext: Reading and learning.* Portsmouth, NH: Heinemann.

Fisher, D., Frey, N., & Hattie, J. (2016). *Visible learning for literacy, grades K–12: Implementing the practices that work best to accelerate student learning.* Thousand Oaks, CA: Corwin.

Fountas, I., & Pinnell, G. S. (2001). *Guiding readers and writers, grades 3–6: Teaching comprehension, genre, and content literacy.* Portsmouth, NH: Heinemann.

Freebody, P., & Luke, A. (1990). "Literacies" programs: Debates and demands in cultural context. *Prospect: An Australian Journal of TESOL, 5*(3), 7–16.

Hagood, M. C., Alvermann, D. E., & Heron-Hruby, A. (2010). *Bring it to class: Unpacking pop culture in literacy learning.* New York: Teachers College Press.

Hancock, M. R. (1993). Exploring the meaning-making process through the content of literature response journals: A case study investigation. *Research in the Teaching of English, 27*(4), 335–68.

Jaeger, E. L. (2015). Literacy and vulnerability: Shame or growth for readers who struggle. *Talking Points, 26*(2), 17–25.

Jewitt, C., & Kress, G. (Eds.) (2003). *Multimodal literacy.* New York: Peter Lang.

Johnson, E. (2014). Reconceptualizing vulnerability in personal narrative writing with youths. *Journal of Adolescent & Adult Literacy, 57*(7), 575–83.

Johnston, P. H. (2004). *Choice words: How our language affects children's learning.* Portland, ME: Stenhouse.

Jones, S., Clarke, L. W., & Enriquez, G. (2010). *The reading turn-around: A five-part framework for differentiated instruction.* New York: Teachers College Press.

Kesler, T., Gibson, L., & Turansky, C. (2016). Bringing the book to life: Responding to historical fiction using digital storytelling. *Journal of Literacy Research, 48*(1), 39–79.

Kesler, T., Tinio, P. P. L., & Nolan, B. T. (2016). What's our position? A critical media literacy study of popular culture websites with eighth-grade special education students. *The Reading & Writing Quarterly, 32*(1), 1–26. doi:10.1080/10573569.2013.857976

Kress, G. (2000). Design and transformation: New theories of meaning. In B. Cope & M. Kalantzis (Eds.), *Multiliteracies: Literacy learning and the design of social futures* (pp. 153–61). London: Routledge.

Leigh, S. R. (2010). Violent red, ogre green, and delicious white: Expanding meaning potential through media. *Language Arts, 87*(4), 252–62.

Leu, D. J., Forzani, E., Rhoads, C., Maykel, C., Kennedy, C., & Timbrell, N. (2015). The new literacies of online research and comprehension: Rethinking the reading achievement gap. *Reading Research Quarterly, 50*(1), 37–60.

Lewison, M., Flint, A. S., & Van Sluys, K. (2002). Taking on critical literacy: The journey of newcomers and novices. *Language Arts, 79*(5), 382–92.

McLaughlin, M., & DeVoogd, G. L. (2004). *Critical literacy: Enhancing students' comprehension of text.* New York: Scholastic.

Newkirk, T. (2009). *Holding on to good ideas in a time of bad ones: Six literacy principles worth fighting for.* Portsmouth, NH: Heinemann.

Partnership for Assessment of Readiness for College and Careers (PARCC). (2011). *PARCC model content frameworks: English language arts/literacy, grades 3–11.* Retrieved from https://eric.ed.gov/?id=ED526347

RAND Reading Study Group. (2002). *Reading for understanding: Toward an R&D program in reading comprehension.* Retrieved from http://www.rand.org/pubs/monograph_reports/MR1465.html

Rief, L. (2007). *Inside the writer's-reader's notebook.* Portsmouth, NH: Heinemann.

Romano, T. (2013). *Fearless writing: Multigenre to motivate and inspire.* Portsmouth, NH: Heinemann.

Rosenblatt, L. M. (1938/1995). *Literature as exploration* (5th ed.). New York: Modern Language Association.

Short, K. G., Harste, J. C., with Burke, C. (1996). *Creating classrooms for authors and inquirers* (2nd ed.). Portsmouth, NH: Heinemann.

Siegel, M. (2006). Rereading the signs: Multimodal transformations in the field of literacy education. *Language Arts, 84*(1), 65–77.

Smagorinsky, P. (2001). If meaning is constructed, what is it made from? Toward a cultural theory of reading. *Review of Educational Research, 71*(1), 133–69.

Smith, F. (1988). *Joining the literacy club: Further essays into education.* Portsmouth, NH: Heinemann.

Suhor, C. (1984). Towards a semiotics-based curriculum. *Journal of Curriculum Studies, 16*(3), 247–57.

Vygotsky, L. S. (1978). *Mind in society: The development of higher psychological processes.* Cambridge, MA: Harvard University Press.

Wertsch, J. V. (1991). *Voices of the mind: A sociocultural approach to mediated action.* Cambridge, MA: Harvard University Press.

Children's Literature Cited

Abbott, T. (2008). *Firegirl.* New York: Little, Brown.

Bash, B. (1989). *Desert giant: The world of the saguaro cactus.* San Francisco: Sierra Club Books.

Boelts, M., & Jones, N. Z. (2007). *Those shoes.* Cambridge, MA: Candlewick Press.

Buyea, R. (2011). *Because of Mr. Terupt.* New York: Yearling.

Carlson, N. S., & Williams, G. (1989). *The family under the bridge.* New York: HarperCollins.

Chibbaro, J., & Sovak, J-M S. (2012). *Deadly.* New York: Atheneum Books.

Curtis, C. P. (1995). *The Watsons go to Birmingham—1963.* New York: Delacorte Press.

DeJong, M. (1972). *The wheel on the school.* New York: HarperCollins.

DePaola, T. (1979). *Oliver Button is a sissy.* New York: Voyager.

DiCamillo, K. (2000). *Because of Winn-Dixie.* Cambridge, MA: Candlewick Press.

DiCamillo, K. (2006). *The tiger rising.* Cambridge, MA: Candlewick Press.

Erskine, K. (2011). *Mockingbird.* New York: Scholastic.

Facklam, M., & Facklam, P. (1994). *The big bug book.* Boston: Little, Brown.

Fleming, C. (2003). *Ben Franklin's almanac: Being a true account of the good gentleman's life.* New York: Atheneum.

Gaiman, N. (2012). *Coraline.* New York: HarperCollins.

Gale, E. K. (2013). *The bully book.* New York: HarperCollins.

Gerstein, M. (2003). *The man who walked between the towers.* New York: MacMillan.

Guiberson, B. Z., & Lloyd, M. (1991). *Cactus hotel.* New York: Henry Holt.

Hannigan, K. (2004). *Ida B . . . and her plans to maximize fun, avoid disaster, and (possibly) save the world.* New York: HarperCollins.

Hermes, P. (2002). My America Series: *Our strange new land: Elizabeth's Jamestown Colony diary, Book 1.* New York: Scholastic.

Hiaasen, C. (2009). *Scat.* New York: Knopf.

Hunter, E., & Stevenson, D. (2015). Warriors: The Prophecies Begin Series: Vol. 2. *Warriors: Fire and ice.* New York: HarperCollins.

Johnston, T., & Mazellan, R. (2004). *The harmonica.* Watertown, MA: Charlesbridge.

Kinney, J. (2007). Diary of a Wimpy Kid Series: Vol. 1. *Diary of a wimpy kid.* New York: Abrams.

Kinney, J. (2014). Diary of a Wimpy Kid Series: Vol.9. *The long haul.* New York: Abrams.

Merrill, J., & Solbert, R. (1964/2015). *The pushcart war.* New York: New York Review of Books.

Milton, S., with Soares, P., Jr., & Maron, J. (2014). *Minecraft: Essential handbook.* New York: Scholastic.

Mitchell, M. K., & Ransome, J. (1998). *Uncle Jed's barbershop.* New York: Aladdin.

Mlynowski, S. (2014). Whatever After Series: Vol. 6. *Cold as ice.* New York: Scholastic.

Mochizuki, K., & Lee, D. (1993). *Baseball saved us.* New York: Lee and Low.

Palacio, R. J. (2012). *Wonder.* New York: Knopf.

Park, B. (2002). *The graduation of Jake Moon.* New York: Aladdin.

Pearsall, S. (2006). *All of the above.* New York: Little, Brown.

Riordan, R. (2008). Percy Jackson and the Olympians Series: Vol. 4. *The battle of the labyrinth.* New York: Hyperion.

Russell, R. R. (2010). Dork Diaries Series: Vol. 1. *Tales from a not-so-fabulous life.* New York: Aladdin.

Speare, E. G. (1983). *The sign of the beaver.* Boston: Houghton Mifflin.

Steptoe, J. (1986). *Stevie.* New York: Harper Trophy.

Strong, J., & Clifford, R. (2015). *Romans on the rampage!* London: Puffin.

Van Allsburg, C. (1991). *The wretched stone.* Boston: Houghton Mifflin.

Wagner, J. (1972). *J.T.* New York: Yearling.

White, E. B. (1952). *Charlotte's web.* New York: Harper Trophy.

Wilder, L. I. (1937/2008). Little House Series: Vol. 3. *On the banks of Plum Creek.* New York: HarperCollins.

Wiles, D., & Lagarrigue, J. (2001). *Freedom summer.* New York: Aladdin.

Index

The letter *f* following a page number denotes a figure. Strategies are found in *italics*.

Author

Ted Kesler taught grades kindergarten, 1, 3, and 4 in New York City public schools. In 1996–97, he was the featured teacher in a nine-part, yearlong series of articles in the *New York Times* called "Class 3-223: Mr. Kesler's Struggle." In 1998 he received the Bank Street College Early Childhood Teacher of the Year Award, and in 2001, he earned National Board for Professional Teaching Standards certification as a middle grades generalist. Kesler is currently an associate professor in literacy at Queens College,

CUNY, where he co-directs the graduate preservice program for elementary grades 1–6 and directs the sabbatical program. He does consulting work in schools and school districts around the country, and his published work has appeared in *The Reading Teacher, Language Arts, The Elementary School Journal, Reading and Writing Quarterly, Children's Literature in Education,* and *Journal of Literacy Research,* among other journals. Visit him at www.tedsclassroom.com and @tedsclassroom.

This book was typeset in TheMix and Palatino by Barbara Frazier.

Typefaces used on the cover include Luxi and Helvetica.

The book was printed on 60-lb. White Offset paper by Versa Press, Inc.